The Deculturalisation
of the English People

The Revd John Lovejoy

Athelney

Published 2000 by
Athelney
1 Providence Street
King's Lynn
Norfolk
England

© The Revd John Lovejoy 2000

Printed by
Antony Rowe Ltd.
Bumper's Farm
Chippenham
Wiltshire SN14 6LH
England

A CIP catalogue record for this book
is available from the British Library.

Contents

A Paradox

Years of travelling may bring
surprising results, wholly unforeseen

Without doubt, I began life with a certain restlessness, for while it is true that I was born in England, of English parents, this was nevertheless at a time and place which were far from auspicious. I began life in East Dulwich, South East London, during the pre-war depression, and the area was heavily bombed, so that it was no doubt a good thing that my parents had decided to move to Sutton, on the Southern outskirts of London, during my first months of life. It was not a good part of Sutton. It was a new street, filled with people from 'The Provinces', who had strange accents, and we were mutual and somewhat distrustful strangers. The street was adjacent to what became a Council tip during the war and my path to school led through a Victorian gas-works, under pipes that leaked smelly chemicals. But that was only after my first school premises was bombed.

Curiously, it was due to the Luftwaffe that I was sent for a while to Cornwall, where I ran rather wild, but had to work on the farm: a farm, be it noted, that had no tractors, but horse-drawn wooden wagons which were in far worse repair than the ones of Constable's famous painting. Cornwall, even at that age, gave me a curious sense of being outside England, but the experience was beneficial. Just after the war, I had another much-needed experience of rural beauty, but this time in the much more English setting of Windsor Great Park, as I stayed with an aunt whose husband worked as a gardener on the Royal Estates. I cannot overestimate the dramatic effect that this interlude had on the consciousness of one who had grown up, except for the period noted above, in the shadow of Sutton gas-works. Among the ancient trees and bracken-bestrewn slopes of the Royal Park, a love of something essentially English was instilled into me, I think. And there, too, I recall that at the tender age of eleven I fell in love.

But something else happened, too, during those early days of childhood, and it was an element of the restlessness which I mentioned at the beginning, a certain looking to distant horizons. In part, of course, this was due to the dreariness of my immediate surroundings, and to the fact that I was rather a bookish only child. But in addition to that, I allowed to grow

5

within me a strong fascination with The North. I found northern friends in the street. At the grammar school which I later attended in Croydon I found a constant friend whose family were from Newcastle upon Tyne. They returned North during my last years at school, and I well remember the journey North along the old A1 on a coach that took twelve hours to arrive! Each pair of passengers had a blanket issued to them to keep off the night chill. I had been joined by a seventeen-year-old young lady who was the last to board the bus, but I can report that her behaviour was impeccable! Anyway, my love of The North was certainly reinforced then, and also later when the same family moved to Cumbria, where I then had a base for exploring the Lake District after finals at the conclusion of student days at King's College London.

The Dean of King's at that time, Sydney Hall Evans, had gathered that I had a love of The North, and so it was that, after a year of post-graduate training in Warminster, I was sent to Newcastle East-End Riverside, to the late-Victorian cobbled streets – all gas-lit when I arrived – of Byker. I was an assistant curate in the Anglican Church, and I began work with genuine culture shock, encountering the full force of the archaic and very musical dialect of that place. There was also an extended family network which seemed to make of the area one huge tribe, and this was the antithesis of what I had grown up with in Sutton.

Much as I loved the riverside area, I also took to exploring the County of Northumberland on my day off. It is a county full of hidden surprises, and much of it has the feeling of being remote and on the very edge of England. Many areas of the County are, indeed, far less accessible to public transport than they were early in the century, when branch railway lines and rural buses extended to most places of consequence. The place-names are steadfastly Anglian, with Bellingham, Eglingham, Whittingham and others all being pronounced with a '-djam' at the end.

After three years I went further North to Choppington, in Bedlingtonshire as some still know it. Ancient family names of Northumbrian sort abounded everywhere, and a few of them astonished me. Visiting one housing area I met a man with un-Northumbrian features and large arched eyebrows. His name was Trevithick. It transpired that his great-great grandfather, a Cornishman, had invented an early form of the steam locomotive. Indeed, in Choppington lies The Wagonway, the site of one of the oldest railway tracks ever. But then, on another housing estate I met individuals with the name Cadwallender – spelt thus. The only likely explanation of this, as I see it in view of the local spelling, is that they are descendants of stragglers from Cadwallader's army, defeated at the Battle of Heavenfield.

So I lived out my love of The North in those days. But this is not an autobiography, and so I must pass over much of personal interest simply by saying that I got married during my time in the North East, but very sadly the marriage broke down, for reasons which I have never entirely been able to fathom.

However, the old restlessness was reawoken by these events, and early in 1970 I decided, in consultation with the Anglican Bishop of Durham, to seek alternative employment overseas for an indeterminate period. I think that I had the notion that, faced with the challenge of rebuilding my life in a new and strange setting, I would be able to reach a new inner equilibrium and deeper personal maturity. Something like that, anyway. In hindsight, I think I can now say that my years of travelling eventually had results which greatly deepened my ties with my land and people of origin rather than the reverse, and now I must explain what I mean. It would seem that the further I got from England, the more I was to discover Englishness. This was the paradox which unfolded itself.

Nigeria
A land of many religions and contrasting identities

Resigning from full-time paid work in the Church, I worked for a while on North Shields Fish-Quay, and then New Malden in South London in a parking-meter factory. There, I met one Sampson Okpodu, a Nigerian, who urged me to consider going to Nigeria, and so I did, as a teacher in the Mid-West State for two years. I had no orientation course, and I was rather vague about where on the map the country was till I arrived there. And the Biafra War had not long finished.

I had two placings during the two years I was there, at a boys' school first, and then, in the second year, a girls' college run by Irish R.C. sisters. I was not teaching English as a subject, but I did note that the students had to read things like Northanger Abbey, which might have occasioned difficulty in some parts of England! The Nigerians have their own somewhat aberrant dialect of English, which they need as there are so many languages within the Federation.

But on me, Nigeria made two sets of very vivid and powerful impressions, first in the local villages of the Ishan Division of the Mid-West State, and then more widely as I began to travel around the Federation during the vacations.

Locally, I came to realise that much survived from what had been essentially a Neolithic culture which had received bronze and iron-age accretions during the most recent millennia. Slavery and smallpox had done their worst, and then there was the most obvious physical result of the colonial period, the replacement of vast areas of primary forest by rubber plantations which, in turn, had been allowed to revert to secondary forest. The area was superabundant in things to eat, and the rainy season never seemed to fail. However, disease was rife and malaria in particular.

The life of the local villages had a very vigorous cultural pattern, according to which 'people' the locals belonged to, each with their own customs, festivals, family structure and distinct language. The Mid-West had a plethora of languages. A person – such as my cook, Andrew – might travel widely, but he would never lose his attachment to his own people, birthplace and village. The agricultural festivals had their own ancient calendar, and seemed to occur in a manner unconnected with the modern calendar and the modern seven-day week. When these festivals occurred, there would be dancing till late around a large wood fire, with a sort of singing in which a haunting and really beautiful melody was repeated for a very long time. I am afraid I have no place for music with Black-American roots, but this music from rural Nigeria drew me powerfully.

Then there were my journeys around the Federation. I will not recount the hair-raising adventures which I had, some of which might have done justice to Indiana Jones, and I reckon that I was lucky to get out alive! But I wanted to observe everything I encountered, and there was much for me to take in. There is an amazing variety of terrain and climate within Nigeria. The ultra-humid and swampy Niger Delta; the somewhat drier and cooler forested zone like the one where my station was situated farther North; the Central Plateau with its poor soils and harsh rocky contours; the vast semi-desert areas of the North. Then there was a little known highland area in the far East of Nigeria which had been the northern section of the German Cameroon in colonial times. Here, I found the Mambilla Plateau, where there was clean, fresh water from mountain streams and a forestry of a more temperate climate, managed at that time by Canadian expatriates. Here, I crossed a crocodile-infested river using liana vine.

The human variety, culturally and even racially, matched the range of terrain. Yoruba in the South West, Igbo in the South-East, along with the many peoples and languages of the Mid-West and the Delta area, such as Esan and Ijaw. In the North, there were the Hausa, who were largely cattlemen, wiry in build and fiery in temperament. The Plateau, to which Jos was the gateway, was the home of very archaic human cultures. The remoter areas of the North-East, around Maiduguri, had different people again, towards the shores of Lake Chad. Religions, too, were diverse, with Islam dominant in the North, and different rites of Christianity in the South, but indigenous religions were also very much alive, and syncretistic cults could also be found. I could not always tell whether some of the strange ceremonies that I stumbled across on occasion were religious in character, or whether they were simply cultural celebrations or re-enactments. The distinction is bound to be blurred.

What did I learn from all this rich and contrasting human diversity? I think that even then I came to understand that the diversity was highly necessary from a human point of view: that is, that the plurality of human cultures, each with its own integrity and aspects of excellence, was something which ought not to be lost, however much a veneer of modernity might supervene. I began to see that the human richness in all its various modes, themselves required in part by the diversities of terrain and climate, was something which was necessarily received from a remoter past, and that human cultures, while they may be transmuted from time to time, must never be diminished or changed in such a way as to alienate them from themselves.

What I did not realise then at all clearly, although the penny was to drop later, is that the lessons which I was confronted with at that time so urgently and vividly also applied elsewhere, and not least to England and to my own people, the English! Let us consider. England is so called because the main southern part of Britain was invaded and settled in the early fifth century – if not before that in some cases – by groups of closely related Germanic peoples whose principal appellation was *Englisc*. But the land which they took control of was, and is, a land of amazing contrasts. As you proceed from the South East to the North West you encounter about every sort of geological stratum imaginable, and when the English arrived there were vast areas of forest and fen, with drainage systems that have since undergone extensive modification. Furthermore, there are surprising contrasts of climate in England for such a relatively small territory. England rests on a transition zone between continental and Atlantic weather systems, and our northerly latitude, while mild because of the Gulf Stream, nevertheless leads to a very significant temperature gradation from south to north, and also with changes of altitude, so that people have to exercise caution in moorland and upland areas.

But it is not just the land which offers these contrasts. I have already remarked the regional distinctions of dialect and custom which I encountered while very young, first because of the drift to the Capital during the 'thirties, and then when I transferred my attentions to the North, though not without some contact with the West during National Service and in my post-graduate year. Of course, the human diversity – at any rate among the English themselves – was never anywhere near as great as in Nigeria, for the simple reason that the English have always been essentially one people even though not at first politically united in one kingdom. I can say, however, that English diversity, up to the time of my youth, was something which was perceived as being remarkable, even without considering the Celtic areas beyond.

There is a sense in which England is a bit like Dr. Who's *tardis*, in that what looks like a small land on the global atlas nevertheless seems to contain long distances and a number of areas that feel remote, and not easy to reach. Our time-scale, too, is impressive. Over a third of our recorded history in this land lies before the cataclysmic, but not definitive, Norman Conquest. And we know that we have a continental pre-history before that. The Old English language itself contains some enigmatic clues. Our word 'butter', for instance, which Old English seems to have inherited from Primitive Germanic, indicating a contact with The Greeks at a very early date, and the languages are cognate in any case, though distantly.

Italy – A country and people with cultural continuity and cultural awareness

I chose not to return to Nigeria, mainly because school-teaching is not my natural mode of life, and after some casting around for a sense of direction in England, and spending time on international work camps, I travelled by train to Milan, and found work in a language school, teaching English.

Milan impressed me heavily in a variety of ways. There was the wealth of impressive architecture in the Centre, and the array of cultural activities and art forms proper to an Italian city. The trams drew my attention, too, and I found that I could stand dreamily on the rear platform, watching a leafy avenue recede from me as I stared from this smoothly moving rail-car, which made but a pleasant, if plaintive, wailing sound, punctuated by a clanging bell. There were, too, the *piazze*, for whereas in modern England you find a traffic junction, period, in Milan as elsewhere on the Continent the junction revolves round an impressive edifice commemorating some momentous event in the nation's history, and on the periphery you will find more than one *bar-cafe* where people of like mind can meet and exchange thoughts on all topics of interest to them.

The cumulative effect on my mind, at that time, was a shaking-up of my imagination of something like seven on the mental Richter Scale. I began to realise consciously what I had been learning unwittingly in Nigeria. I started to make a personal critique of the Modern Civilisation (to use a deliberately vague term). I discovered the Green Movement for myself, as I had not then realised that it had already come into being, and I became aware of a number of things in the Modern Civilisation which I could now see were increasingly dangerous.

In fact, I began to ask the question 'What do we mean by a human 'culture', or 'civilisation'? On these themes I started to write reams of stuff to my friends in England.

At that time, of course, I had little opportunity of applying what I was learning to the situation in England itself, although one thing helped, and that was my paid job in TEFL, which led me to examine the character and structure of the modern English language in its received standard British-English form. I was fascinated by it, and increasingly impressed. The English Principal of the language school, before he retired, reminded me that Modern English was demonstrably descended from the Old English language, 'Anglo-Saxon' as we both then called it, and thus was sown the seed of a later increasing interest in the Old form – *Englisc*.

While in Milan, I came to believe that in England there was a relatively high cultural impoverishment, this being due, I thought, to a number of related factors, such as strong class divisions, the early arrival of the Industrial Revolution in its earliest and crudest form, the element of utilitarianism in nineteenth-century philosophical thinking, the concentration of effort into expanding and maintaining the Empire, and the effect of two World Wars. Moreover, the high degree of fragmentation of the prevailing religion meant, I saw, that the modern English lacked an advantage which Greece, Poland, and even Norway, seem to have had, when it comes to encouragement of cultural continuity and integrity – not to mention Italy.

Algiers
A city with deep scars and communal fault-lines

After two years I left Italy, and after a visit to the UK made my way to Milan only to leave immediately for Marseilles, whence I took a crossing by sea to Algiers. I arrived at the seaport only to find the place utterly deserted, so I simply walked into the Country, though one man did appear after a bit to stamp my passport. I had arrived on the first Friday which was being observed officially and nationally as the day of rest in that country!

I did find the Language School, and two Irish members of staff were waiting for me to accompany me to my apartment. I have to say that I had rather an uncomfortable time in Algiers, and after a while I began to see why. The war of independence which ended with the Treaty of Evian was not as simple as it seems. Besides the independence issue was the tension between mainland France and the *pied-noirs*; and between Arab and Berber. The Berbers refused, in many instances, even to learn the Arabic alphabet. Unable to use their own language publicly, they used French. Another alarming trend was the population explosion in this previously very French city. There was also a growing tension, even then, between those who practised a rather nominal form of Islam, and those who wanted something dogmatic and thoroughgoing.

I am not sure what all this was teaching me in a more general way, but two separate incidents are worthy of note.

One day, I was rummaging round in the rear of a newly reopened shop near the Casbah. It was a Bible Shop, and Government permission had been granted. To my astonishment, in the dust and gloom of an old cupboard, I found some old printing plates bearing a script which I had never before seen. It dawned on me that they were in the old Berber script and language, which were both politically suppressed at that time. We had them spirited away – I am not sure where! Looking at the script at the time, I thought it was not far removed from the ancestral Phoenician script

12

which, I think, underlies a number of modern alphabets. Perhaps, here, is an impulse to the study of indigenous scripts in general, and to *futhorc*[1] which we are rediscovering slowly, in the case of *Englisc*.

The other event concerned a visit I made to the British Council library in Algiers. I was looking for language material, as I was still teaching in my first year in the city. My eye alighted on a copy of *Teach Yourself Old English*, by Leslie Blakeley. I have to confess – and I was forty-two at the time – that I really had not been aware before that, that the old language was currently accessible for study! Nobody at school, at any level, had ever referred to the Old English language, though there was once a rather half-hearted attempt I recall to introduce us to the Middle-English of Chaucer.

Apart from making me want to begin learning Old English, it also made me ask myself why there was such a low level of awareness, among modern English people, of the existence and present available status of Old English as a classical language. It could well be that to increase the level of awareness of the Old English language will be a principal way of raising awareness of the Old English period and its culture generally. I rather think so, for this can operate even where there is no desire to learn the language. Even to see Old English written down, whether in *futhork*, Insular Script, or an editor's preferred convention for the use of the modern alphabet, is a powerful reminder of the people and the times when the language was in daily use.

Well, I did discover Old English for myself in the end. But in Algiers?

The Kimberley Plateau, North West Australia
A Dreamtime Fastness

I remained no longer in Algiers than in Milan, but the impetus to my imagination continued, and I developed a desire to have contact with an archaic tribal people. I returned to the UK long enough to research possibilities, and eventually found a post in the far North West of Australia which involved commuting between the township of Wyndham on the

---

[1] The *futhorc* is an English version of the runic alphabet, and is so named after the first six runic letters in the sequence; just as *alphabet* is constructed from the first two letters, *alpha* and *beta*, in the Greek sequence of letters.

Cambridge Gulf and Oombulgurri, which was an Aboriginal station on the Forrest River.

I did not succeed in doing very much either to or for the Aborigines, and this was no doubt a good thing, for these unfortunate people had had more than enough of people doing things to or for them. I wanted to learn from them, and had to be prepared for them to make things known to me in their own time and in their own way. I had been hoping to help them to recover the local language, and reduce it to a written form, but unfortunately I was, I estimate, some ten years too late for that. This should remind us how fortunate we are, in England, to have written records in the Old English language, for *Englisc* has had to reach us through centuries of indifference and neglect. The same could be said of the Celtic languages, I suppose, including in their case the modern form as well.

It will be asked what sort of things I learnt from the Aborigines, and in what ways they reinforced what I already knew. I will list the main things now.

1. A land where Mesolithic cultures survived intact till very recently

The Aborigines, generally, were what we might call Middle Stone Age peoples. We may also use the term 'archaic tribal people'. But these are our terms, not theirs, and there are faults in our perspective, for the nineteenth century concept of 'Progress' has bitten very deep into our thinking and conceptual system. Aboriginal societies in Australia were just as complete, as valid human cultures, as our own, and in many ways, perhaps, even more so. It is just that they travelled light through this world, and such technology as they had was for the most part within their heads. They exercised the cultural choice of fitting in with the environment, rather than harnessing it, exploiting it, taming it.

This is important for us because it is probable that the whole human race passed through a Mesolithic phase over a very long time period, and that the Aborigines of Australia were unusual only because they persisted longer in that phase. I do not think that the peoples who spoke the Primitive Germanic language could have been far removed from Mesolithic culture, because words which the Neolithic peoples would have found useful seem often to be other than Indo-European. Be that as it may, Mesolithic cultures in general show us a lot about the central stuff of raw humanity in an archaic presentation.

These archaic Mesolithic peoples tend to concentrate on the things that really matter, and I list:–

- The 'Dreamtime' and the Ancient 'Law', in which a system of mythology will have been handed down from remote antiquity, in such a way as to underpin a current religious system and a communal code of behaviour, governing all areas of communal life.

- The relationship with the territory, whereby the particular people in question inherits a system of communal survival within the territory to which they belong and to which they have always belonged.

- The Relationship System, whereby human relationships of various degrees are regulated according to the requirements of the archaic Law – albeit with some flexibility – so as to form a communal pattern of interwoven types and degrees of relationship, modulated by differences of sex and age. The relationship system serves as the political system in these archaic societies.

- The Initiation Ceremonies. Social Anthropologists delight in studying the *rites of passage*, and I will not dwell on this point in detail because my experience was with a culture which was extremely fractured anyway. But I will make the point that the near-universal occurrence of these things in archaic societies suggests that any society which omits them in any form does so at its communal peril, and is not a complete human society.

- The Language. I have already mentioned my relative failure in trying to recover one such, but there was another difficulty which I only realised towards the end of my time among the people of Oombulgurri. I asked one older man why it was so hard to recover the old language, and he replied only with hesitance, at first simply scratching strange patterns on the sand at our feet. The gist of his reply, though, which I did elicit this time, was that the old language was regarded as part and parcel with the Ancient Law, and the terms of the Ancient Law were very largely broken now. The Aborigines were no longer able to live according to the Ancient Law in its entirety, and so the use of the old language would have been too uncomfortable a reminder of this fact.

Such were the main elements of the archaic cultures, the details of which were filled in culture by culture. A realisation of these things in Old English studies will help to give us a better perspective. Instead of comparing Anglo-Saxon society with what we have now (whatever that really is), we can ask instead how Old English society differed from the archaic tribal societies from which we are all descended anyway. Further, in that the archaic societies supply us with a list of the really basic and fundamental questions of human existence, we can then ask how the Old English people managed to address the same fundamental human issues in practice.

2. The importance of the persistence of human cultures over long periods of time

The Mesolithic cultures of Australia present us with cultural continuity and persistence in what, to our modern perspective, seems an extreme form. We may believe that change did occur, but that this probably happened in cycles, reversibly, according to fluctuations of the Earth's climatic systems and orbital variations. There is no answer to the question 'When was the Dreamtime?', for archaic societies did not have the sense of history unfolding in an ever-extending chronology or events. Perhaps the ancient myths do present us with symbolic representations of cataclysmic events in a very remote past, but we have no means of unlocking such symbolism. Rather, we have to see the 'Dreamtime' as being effectively outside time, and the myths have to be viewed in terms of their present functions.

This said, we can assume that the aboriginal societies have persisted for many tens of thousands of years, without dramatic changes, and since this must have been the case elsewhere in the world once upon a time, we may be led to think that human beings need cultural continuity, and that rapid and accelerating change may be extremely bad for us in ways that we do not realise.

In Old English times, there were relatively stable periods, and there were other times when change and instability were forced on them from outside, either by invasion, or by famine and pestilence. The Seventh Century conversion was a change, but the impact on the shape and form of Old English society may be less than a lot of people suppose. It seems to me likely that the Christian Faith, in the form that it took then, for the most part filled the gaps which the retreat of the Old Religion had left. But we live in a part of the world which seems prone to change, and so we have to be quite specific as to the period we mean when we are talking about the characteristics of Old English society. But that said, the people who lived in the Old English times would not have experienced change in the relentless, ongoing and accelerating way that it has taken in our own times. Rather, there would have been cataclysmic events from time to time, followed by periods of slow return to a normality which would be in certain respects different from the previous *status quo*.

3. The importance of plurality and diversity for human societies

Australia is an island continent, and is about the same size as the U.S.A. if we leave Alaska out of account. There was no 'Aboriginal Society', anymore than there is a 'European Society', for the land as a whole comprises many climates and types of terrain, so that the Mesolithic societies, which by definition mould themselves to the particular terrain in which they live, differ from one another quite remarkably. Although I worked in the Kimberley, I was able to meet, from time to time, some of the Desert Aborigines, for they were often picked up after drunken brawls, and left to sober up in Wyndham Jail, which was effectively a drying-out centre. Indeed, it is the only jail I know where the perimeter fence was intended to keep people out rather than in. The Desert Aborigines were racially markedly different from the peoples of the Kimberley Plateau.

Now there is strong evidence that Australia, in recent prehistoric times has had progressive changes of climate. That is why, as my own father remarked during a visit to South West Australia in 1982, the trees seem to be struggling to survive. Australian trees often do better in another country.

Meanwhile, human societies have also had to adapt to the changes of the last tens of thousands of years, and a plurality of human cultures offered the best chance of survival for the human population as a whole.

When we consider the case of Old English society, it can hardly be a matter of regret that the political unification of England took so long to bring about. Old English society must have been all the more vigorous because of the juxtaposition of the different kingdoms. On the other hand, it might also be argued that the Old English kingdoms would have done well to have learned earlier how to co-operate against a common external foe, as was the case with the Hellenic societies of Ancient Greece. Classical Greece, one supposes, was always united in some degree by the Aegean Sea, rather than by land, and perhaps the English needed to have

17

maintained longer their recognised early prowess in ship construction and seamanship.

4. An Aboriginal nightmare – the loss of their womenfolk

When I arrived in Oombulgurri, I suppose that even I was hoping for things to happen. They didn't. Only, every time the Unemployment Benefit cheques arrived in Wyndham, the Aboriginal men went by charter plane to Wyndham and went in for bouts of heavy drinking, after first getting rid of the cash at the Liquor Store.

For a long time I tried to puzzle out why this self-destructiveness was so pervasive amongst the whole male population of a certain age-group, and among a lesser number of the women. The usual explanation was that the ancient culture had been smashed by the arrival of the cattle industry in the North, and the archaic tribal Law was no longer operative in its entirety. This is no doubt true in some measure, but human societies can recover from a great deal of disruption, and I think that the Old English culture could be cited as an example.

It was when I returned to modern England that the main explanation became clear to me. The cattlemen, earlier in the century, had not only shot up the Aborigines on occasion, when they hunted across the European men's boundaries, but they did something worse. They did employ the Aborigines as stockmen, but there was a terrible price to pay, for the women began to yearn for the things which the Europeans had, and the Europeans used the Aboriginal women for sexual relief. No further explanation is needed for pervasive alcoholic destructiveness which I saw. The men had been losing their own womenfolk, and life became a nightmare from which they saw alcohol (in the form of cheap port) as the only escape. I hope that the human race as a whole has learned better by now, but I doubt it.

5. The beginnings of cultural reconstruction

The last section was rather a sombre one, but I was with the Aboriginal community at a difficult time. When I visited them later during a Christmas vacation after I returned to Australia to work in Perth, I saw many signs of hope. A new generation was now growing up which wanted some thing different from the alcoholic despair of their fathers and uncles. Western Australia began to take a live interest in the Community Special School, and sent a supply of teachers who were sympathetic to Aboriginal culture, and knew what they were doing. And then, there were the children themselves. In many ways they took their own education in hand. When I arrived on the visit, the children took me to a waterfall as the rainy season was beginning, and got me to jump off cliffs into the rock-pool below. These children also have a good sense of humour!

Of course, they cannot go back to the hunter-gatherer existence that their forebears had had, but they can be aware of it; they can be proud of it; and also they can undertake the task of choosing which elements of the old way of life can be combined with elements from the new, in a viable way for the present time. In all this, as a constant background, is the fact that the modern Aboriginal settlement of Oombulgurri lies within the same territory which they always inhabited, and the terrain as a whole, in that wild, remote area, remains largely what it always was, awe-inspiring, humbling to the human spirit, and a challenge to human powers of survival.

Can those with Old English interests find inspiration here? I like to think so. I do believe, along with many, that we are faced in our own day with an immense task of cultural reconstruction, though we can no more go back to the way of life of Old English times than the Aborigines can revert to their ways of before the European settlement.

If I am right, then our task is not entirely dissimilar to that of the Aborigines, in that modern English people, those that is who are culturally aware, need to make themselves familiar with what is known about the Old English times, so that they have the right sort of inspiration for the present activities, drawn from the right sources. Not to do this would be to allow, if only by default, some other source of cultural inspiration to shape and mould our current endeavours of cultural reconstruction. And this is where I see the importance, in large measure, of the studies and activities which Ða Engliscan Gesiðas (The English Companions) engage in, for although their studies are strictly to do with discovery of what is the truth about the Old English period, nevertheless it is modern English people, for the most part, who will be found taking a lively interest in the Anglo-Saxons, their language and culture. People of other ethnic backgrounds would be entirely welcome in Ða Engliscan Gesiðas, I am certain, but I do not see them, and the reason is surely that they are drawn to other sources of inspiration as the founts of their respective cultures.

As a modern Englishman myself, I have believed, since returning to England in recent years, that a movement towards cultural reconstruction among our own ethnic community is both highly desirable and very urgent.

Huntly, West Aberdeenshire
A year in the North-East of Scotland

As this is not an autobiography, I do not have to explain the steps that led me from North West Australia, one of the Earth's hottest places, to the North-East of Scotland, just when a quite severe winter was approaching. Somewhere between, I was on an Archaeological dig near an Anglo-Saxon cemetery, but that is another story. The dig was to have momentous consequences for me later.

But in Strathbogie, as the area around Huntly is known, I was simply impressed by the sheer Scottishness of everything around me: the salmon rivers, the foothills of the North Grampian, the ruined castles, the distilleries, the forests, the granitic architecture, the low clouds. In the smaller villages towards the Grampians the old Doric dialect could be heard; arguably the most archaic surviving form of English, though I should like to know what others think.

I was working for a year as a gardener at the Alexander Scott Memorial Hospital, and was staying in the attic of a massive granite town building in the centre of Huntly, only two doors away from where the well-known writer George MacDonald had once lived. In those days I did watch TV in the evening, to relax.

While viewing in this way one evening in June 1986, I happened to watch an instalment of the series *The Blood of the British* on Channel Four, presented by the archaeologist Catherine Hills. I was horrified to find the view being set forth that the basic identity of the population in Britain remained essentially unchanged, despite some disturbance from some bands of marauders from time to time, the Angles and Saxons being named among them somewhere within a list of relatively unimportant chance newcomers.

This distortion of the facts incensed me so much that I immediately wrote to complain to the Independent Broadcasting Authority, and then set about preparing a large paper on the subject of cultural disintegration and degradation among the modern English People. This paper I then addressed to the then Home Secretary, The Right Hon. Sir Douglas Hurd. And in reply:–

> Thank you for you letter of 29 May to the Home Secretary enclosing your very interesting analysis of a problem facing society today.
>
> Your paper will be studied with care.

I was a little bit worried about the last lines. Was it just me, or was I really being watched for a while after that?

Anyway, there are probably many ways whereby those in power might try to obliterate a nation or ethnic group, but Catherine Hills' method was rather subtle. Using the Broadcast Media, you <u>define</u> a nation out of existence. They never really existed in the first place!

All of which demonstrates a principle which I have in the past discussed with other members (gesiðas) of Ða Engliscan Gesiðas. In that Fellowship, which is strictly non-sectarian and non-political, we strictly avoid involvement in any matters of contention concerning the English People at the present time. But when it comes to attempts to falsify the events of the Old English period, or to inflict damage on the sites dating from those days, then we feel free to raise a voice in protest. That, after all, was how Ða Engliscan Gesiðas started.

After a year, I left Scotland for a while to return to Australia, this time near Perth WA, as I needed to be able to send more money to my two teenage children, and in Western Australia I was able to do so when they needed it.

Perth, Western Australia
Evidence of transferred Englishness

Suddenly arriving on my Aussie cousin's doorstep I found work as quickly as I could, and took employment in an engineering works where we applied rubber linings to steel mining machinery. The work was heavy, noisy, dirty, and dangerous, and I loved it! As I was used largely to assemble the iron-ore screen decks for the Pilbara iron-ore extraction companies, I had rather a central place, I felt, in the Western Australian economy.

All of which might seem irrelevant but for one thing. The works radio, which in any case was usually inaudible because of the much preferable noise of the machinery, was situated inside, whereas I was in the yard at the back, and was free to listen to Radio 6NR, the like of which does not seem to exist in England. Radio 6NR specialised in archaic recordings and music from very early in the 20th century, if not at times from the end of the last one. Thus, truck drivers who rounded the corner into the yard would suddenly hear, *I heard a brown bird singing...*; or *Less than the dust beneath thy chariot wheel...*; or *Come, come, come to me Thora...*; and many other such items from the days of aspidistras, macassar oil, and the Constitutional, as well as The Raj and British naval supremacy. The recordings, of course, were either scratchy 78's if they had not been remastered, or even, in some cases, shellac cylinders.

I had not realised, till then, how averse I had become to Transatlantic Pop in all of its ramifications, and I saw that we have to go back rather a long way to find a time when we were not being overwhelmed by one popular musical form or another from the U.S.A. Not that even what I was hearing on Radio 6NR was without its distortions, from the point of view of someone wanting a truly English popular cultural form. The British Imperial backdrop itself distorted popular musical development, as witness the popularity of Amy Woodforde Finden's *Indian Love Lyrics* and others by Albert Ketelby. Still, I wish I could listen now to Radio 6NR, because I really cannot accept Transatlantic Pop any more: it seems so alien to me, and even downright horrible. I get some relief by listening to LGR (no, not GLR) – London Greek Radio. At least the Greeks remain refreshingly Greek.

Perhaps it was this musical experience which inspired me later, while in Perth WA, to write a leaflet expounding the beginnings and origins of English society and culture, as I wanted a convenient hand-out to use later while on a Long Distance Run which I hoped to do when I arrived back in England. For I had to return in order to begin caring for my increasingly elderly parents by this time, in 1988.

England as I found it on my return to my land of origin, in 1988

Thus, at last I returned to England at the end of the eighties after restless wanderings over many years, after I had found it necessary to leave the North-East, in 1970. I returned with the leaflets which I have mentioned, and with the firm intention of going on Long Distance Runs around England, in the hope of meeting people and awakening an interest in the Old English basis of our identity.

I have to say that at the time when I returned to England, I did not like what I saw. Indeed, I was so disturbed by what I saw around me, or saw and heard on the Broadcast Media, that I started to write papers rather in the vein of the earlier ones that I had written while in Scotland, in Huntly.

Here, I can do no more than to indicate my main areas of disquiet in a series of headings, each of which could have been expanded into the size of a chapter or even a whole book. For this purpose, I continued to use the word *deculturalisation*, a rather appropriately ugly word which I had used in my paper to the Home Secretary, in 1986. The headings which I would use to indicate my main departures of thought at that time were these:-

- Dismay at the extent of deculturalisation in Greater London, among young English people.

- The massive degree of Americanisation of popular culture.

- The disregard of, or attacks on, English culture and origins, on the part of Broadcast Media.

- The evident decay of the Modern English language under the impact of social and economic change, and under foreign influence.

- A near universal amnesia in respect of the Old English period and its culture, among ordinary people.

- The prevalence of double standards, whereby other nations and ethnic communities were often being encouraged in an awareness of identity and cultural expression which was being condemned or denied in the case of the English.

- A refusal to listen to complaints from English people on the part of official agencies and departments, and a lack of any representative voice for English people – this in strong contrast with the clearly evident means of common expression which other ethnic communities had.

In 1989, with this kind of thinking in my mind, I did indeed set off on a series of Long Distance Runs, working my way slowly through England, doing about twenty-five miles per day, and staying overnight in Bed-and-Breakfast accommodation. I found that I could make some of my most valuable contacts with ordinary people when I stopped for lunch, or at breakfast in the B&B place. For the most part, however, I was alone with my own thoughts while running, and the physical effect of running sharpened my imagination and perception so that I was able to appreciate the English scenery and the successive regional characteristics as I passed through them. I was not always able to avoid main roads, but where possible I used a network of minor roads as indicated on a good map and also took local advice about off-route pathways and tracks. National networks are beginning to appear, such as those under the heading of *sustrans*.

I had to stop these activities for a long time because of caring duties at home, but in the meantime I had been receiving a booklist produced by one of the jurisdictions of the Orthodox Church operating in England. Because of the interest that they have in the history of Christianity in England before the Great Schism of 1054, the Orthodox Church included in its booklists some titles produced by Anglo-Saxon Books, and when I actually acquired one of these titles the book contained an advertisement for Ða Engliscan Gesiðas, which I was then able to join.

My discovery of like-minded people in this way was timely, because previously, in my isolation, I had been making some plans to launch an organisation of some sort to promote interest in the beginnings and origins of English culture and national identity, but now it seemed that this was already happening, so I was saved the trouble!

I have mentioned the tangential part that the Orthodox Church played in my discovery of Ða Engliscan Gesiðas through the common interest in the Old English period, and it is not my purpose to discuss matters such as ecclesiastical allegiances, but in fact I did become attached to the Greek Orthodox Church as it operates in this country, and this meant that recently I have had to cope with the Greek language and also make friends with the Greek Community. I have to say that in a place like London the Greek Community sets a very encouraging example in their persistence and determination to maintain their culture and identity, which they value and enjoy tremendously, while living in a setting which, as we know, is becoming increasingly hostile to any such purpose, whether one is Greek or English. I hope it will be understood, then, if I mention my new-found friends.

At one function which I attended when I first contacted the Greeks, I was seated at a table in an upper room of the church building, and on the wall appeared, not holy pictures, but fierce-looking nineteenth-century warriors! The Greeks do have an advantage in that they are able to appeal to recent struggles to survive as a nation, whereas more recent English history has been submerged, rather, in the British Imperial phase of our history. As regards the classical phase of their history, I think that the Greeks have a problem reverse to that of our own, for Classical Greek culture is so famous that it tends to overshadow the present, whereas we are struggling to win recognition for the Old English culture.

I can report that Andreas, my table-companion that evening, recalled the part that Lord Byron played in the history of independence of his people.

In any case, the Greeks have a tremendous advantage in that they have a very distinct language and alphabet, and also have a common religion (as have certain other nations) which serves to cement their culture and social structure. But a lot of the young members of the Greek community no longer speak Greek, and this is becoming a problem. And it is our problem too. What I often hear in the street or on the radio is not what I would recognise as English. While we, in groups such as Ða Engliscan Gesiðas, rightly turn our attention to Old English, I think that it is also right that we should resist the degradation and impoverishment of the modern language in its British form. Other nations and peoples may use English, but surely the English themselves have the right – even a duty – to value and develop their own standard form of the language which took shape among us in the first instance. One's language is a very intimate and integral part of one's humanity.

In all, I am hoping that my attachment to the Greek Community will help me to have a sharper perspective of the problems faced by the English Community as we face the task, as I see it, of cultural reconstruction and reaffirmation of what is ours.

In conclusion – English culture
and identity perceived in many other settings

I began by mentioning the paradox that the further I got from England, the more I was to discover Englishness. Perhaps I should summarize very briefly what I learnt.

In the North-East of England, I was confronted with a lower working-class English society which, at that time, had not undergone the disintegration and fragmentation which I had grown up with in Greater London. This gave me a sense of grief for something lost. I also saw a late form of a strong regional culture.

In Nigeria, especially as I travelled round by pick-up vehicle or motorbike, I came to see the rich diversity of the many regions of that large African country, and my sense that such diversity is fundamentally necessary to humanity was starting to take shape.

In Italy, surrounded by beautiful cultural forms and architecture, as well as by the vivid and expressive language, I began to see the immense importance of cultural integrity, and began to realise that human beings cannot exist without a culture or civilisation to grow up in. I also started to question what the Modern Civilisation was, and what was wrong with it.

In Algiers, besides seeing and sensing the tensions which remained after the recent turmoil surrounding independence, I rediscovered the Old English language in an unlikely place, and – through seeing the contrast between Arabic and Berber – I saw the vital connection between language and culture in that setting.

While with the Aboriginal Community of Oombulgurri, Forest River, NW Australia, I learned to be patient and in that way learned so much.

- I saw, in all its starkness and horror, the effects of cultural devastation and collapse.

- At the same time, much remained under the surface, and I saw the amazing persistence of cultural elements which had been transmitted, one supposes, through many thousands of years.

- There was still an awareness of The Dreamtime, the core and source, mythically expressed, of the people and their culture and of the land to which they belonged, as well as of all the living things on it.

- There was the prominence, as in Mesolithic cultures generally, of those elements of human culture which are vitally important, and which must be successfully addressed in any viable human way of life.

- There was the sad loss of the indigenous language, in that particular instance, along with the development of their own very distinctive Aboriginal dialect of English, retaining much of the phonetic system and many words from the old language.

- Lastly, there was the growing self-confidence of a new generation, with a determination to undertake a cultural reconstruction, using what they could from the past, with such elements of the modern way of life as they would need in order that they might now relate to the world as they found it.

Since all human beings are descended from archaic human societies, it behoves us to learn as much as we can from them and from what has happened to them in the wake of contact with late European societies.

In Scotland, I suppose, I learned to speak up when I began to realise that English culture and identity were being misrepresented. It also occurred to me that the English can only gain from the Scots' own attempts to express their self -awareness and national identity.

And finally, I have been presented with the example of the Greeks, whose own communal determination to express their culture and identity is evident within England itself, and not least within those urban parts of England where the English themselves have suffered most from disintegration of their way of life.

As a result of what I have been able to observe, in all these settings and in many and various ways, I wish now to encourage my own people, the English People, to take heart from what happens elsewhere, but also to lose any complacency which they might have had. Our task is to recover an understanding of what a human society and a human culture truly mean, and then to begin to reconstruct our own English way of life, using whatever we can recover from the Old English period for sources and inspiration, and whatever lessons we may learn from what has happened to other peoples elsewhere, for I believe that the necessary plurality of human cultures is an axiom which we may safely use, and. surely the English culture has its place within that rich patchwork quilt of human ways of life which the human spirit, at its best, has always welcomed and accepted.

Let us recall, too, that cultural reconstruction is not an unprecedented exercise. I would ask my compatriots to read afresh the words of Alfred, King of the West Saxons, as he writes on the state of learning in England in a letter prefixed to his version of Gregory the Great's *Pastoral Care*.

> ða ic ða ðis eall gemunde ða gemunde ic eac hu ic geseah, ærðæmðe hit eall forhergod wære ⁊ forbærned, hu ða ciricean giond eall Angelcynn stodon maðma ⁊ boca gefyldæ ond eac micel menigeo Godes ðiowa ⁊ ða swiðe lytle fiorme ðara boca wiston, forðæmðe hie hiora nan wuht ongiotan ne meahton ond þæt wæs forðæmðe hie næron on hiora agen geðiode awritene. Swelce hie cwæden:
>
> Ure ieldran, ða ðe ðas stowa ær hioldon, hie lufodon wisdom ⁊ ðurh ðone hie begeaton welan ⁊ us læfdon. Her mon mæg giet gesion hiora swæð, ac we him ne cunnon æfterspyrigean, ⁊ forðæm we habbað nu ægðer forlæten ge ðone welan ge ðone wisdom, forðæmðe we noldon to ðæm spore mid ure mode onlutan.
>
> When I reflected on all this, I then recalled how I saw – before it was all plundered and burnt down – how the churches throughout all England stood filled with treasures and books and a great throng of God's servants; and they knew very little benefit from those books, because they could not understand anything in them, for they were not written in their own language. Thus they spoke:
>
> "Our forefathers, who previously held these places, they loved wisdom and through it they came by wealth and left it to us. One can still see their track here, but we cannot follow them for we have now given up both that wealth and that wisdom, because we did not wish to hold to the track with our hearts."
>
> Translation by Stephen Pollington

This chapter has taken the form of a sort of odyssey, I suppose, but this is enough of my travellers' tales and reminiscences from far away and sometimes not so far away.

Perhaps I have had to omit a lot (the good bits?), but then I have not intended to give a continuous connected discourse. Instead, I hope that many of my recollections are relevant, and help to cast light on the English situation from various perspectives.

Currently, at the time of writing, I have to remain where I am as I may be needed in special ways by those who are very close to me, but it is my hope that again, in the not distant future, I may go on Long Distance Runs across England in order to help raise awareness of the Old English basis of our culture and identity as a people and nation.

Along with whatever I may do in that way, it is also my earnest hope that all who hold England dear, and wish to affirm the continued existence of the people who call themselves English, may likewise find ways of rekindling the ardent interest in the beginnings and origins of our people, together with its current expression, which is surely required of us in these days as it was in the days of Alfred Athelwulfing.

The Deculturalisation of the English People

A Paper written in 1986 by The Rev. John Lovejoy and addressed to Sir Douglas Hurd, Secretary of State for the Home Department

Contents

The Deculturalisation
of the English People

The Basic Concept

I must find an easy place to begin to say what I mean. To this end, I refer again to my more recent experience of four and a half years in the Kimberley, in North West Australia, with a largely Aboriginal population. For most of that time I served as a stipendiary priest in the Anglican Church Diocese of North West Australia, although on arrival I was not in full-time paid service but had other paid employment as I have often had and as is the case just now.

It was there, among the Aborigines of the region, that I saw, in an accelerated and concentrated form, a vivid example of the danger of which I am going to speak. In other places, it was true, I had seen the traditional way of life of the local people under the stress and pressure of rapid change, but here was a people whose whole common mode of existence had dramatically collapsed, with results which were harrowing to see, being shown tangibly and visibly in alcoholism, violence, marital irregularity (by anybody's customs), degradation in speech – their own language having been lost beyond recall, and intensive preoccupation with gambling. That was what was observable on the surface. Behind that was the progressive loss the whole mental and conceptual fabric, along with its indigenous spiritual sanctions in mythology, of the way of life which had doubtless enabled them to survive with a complete human existence for tens of millennia.

That was one particularly acute example where a whole people had lost their way of life – with results both ugly and tragic – within a span of time which was almost covered by living memory.

More generally, I now assert that what I observed in one place can happen anywhere. Whatever the part of the world from which Man comes he has the same primary basic needs which must be met. Readily we recognise the physical needs of food, drink, air, shelter; while we also acknowledge quite easily the emotional needs of the individual person for secure bonds of affection and esteem within his immediate relationships.

31

I now want to stress – and this as forcibly as I may – that it is a primary need of the human being that he grow up in and belong to a particular people sharing an inherited patterning of the mind which we call *a culture* or *a civilisation*. Bereft of this, the human individual cannot lead a fully human life. Instead, he will suffer mentally, emotionally, physically, and will become unstable in behaviour in ways which we might well recognise. Human beings are not 'programmed' by a set of genetically inherited instincts, but vitally require the moulding of the mind and spirit that is integral to the process of growing up within any particular civilisation or culture that truly functions as such.

For what I saw, then, in the case of the Aboriginal People of the East Kimberley in North West Australia, and for what can likewise easily happen to Men elsewhere, a single word is needed. That word, fittingly ungainly as it is, is Deculturalisation.

Deculturalisation, therefore, is largely what this letter is about, and it is a frightening disaster, which leaves individual men and women in a conceptual wilderness and in an unresolvable crisis of identity.

The individual can no longer answer such basic questions as:

"Who am I?"   "What are our beliefs?"

"What do I believe?"   'What are our origins"

"Where do I belong?"   "What is our destiny?"

"Who am I loyal to?"

The result of all this is degradation of every conceivable kind, including alcoholism; drug and solvent addiction; breakdown of human relations; violence; the assumption of borrowed mob identities; the decay of the gift of language; and the adoption of a wholly materialistic value system.

If that is all that I had to say, that I had observed these things happening to a small isolated population of erstwhile Mesolithic people on the other side of the world, then I would not be writing this Letter. It would be a matter for a report to be addressed to the Bishop of Northwest Australia and perhaps to be brought to the attention of the respective Governments in Perth W. A. and in Canberra. Such a report I did frame before I left. It was confidential and I did not retain a copy.

What is very much to the point is that when I returned to England, early in 1984, it began to dawn on me that the very same things, in principle, that I had seen in the East Kimberley were also happening to my own people, in my own Country. I am an Englishman. That is the reason for this letter. I wish to make the point very urgently that the English People, of which I am one, are in severe danger of what I have already called deculturalisation.

The Deculturalisation of the English People

I am aware that this is a most astonishing assertion, and I allowed myself plenty of time to make a reasonably balanced assessment of what I found and experienced in England before writing in this manner. For I was in South London for a large part of the time between March 1984 and September 1985. It was only then that I withdrew to the comparative isolation of a remote Aberdeenshire burgh where I enjoy the hospitality of our main sister nation within the Union of Great Britain, and also full-time paid employment as a gardener. I function within the Episcopal Church, but not in a paid capacity.

While in London, I stayed for a considerable time in the London Borough of Sutton, a very mixed area, and North Sutton where I was is arguably not the most salubrious zone of that Borough. Perhaps it was the worst part, but there would be more disturbed areas in Greater London as a whole. In short, North Sutton is fairly typical. Since I have two children in Newcastle-upon-Tyne, visited Manchester for a job interview, and read the best papers assiduously during that time, I could reasonably suppose that I was in a position to get a fairly clear view. Moreover, I had the experience of being on Unemployment Benefit for part of the time, and later of working on a "Community Programme" job, where I met a great assortment of mainly English people who had themselves been unemployed for over a year.

And with the background that I had previously had, I will now set out the specific kinds of distress that I noted during that time. 'Social distress' is the term that one has come to expect here, but if this letter has any valid point to make at all, then 'Anthropological distress' would be at least as appropriate a phrase, and possibly much more so. This, then, is what I found:-

1. A lack of regularity and cohesion in human relationship and in community

Perhaps the fact that I had stayed for three weeks, on my way back from Australia, in the Malaysian Province of Kelantan, made me even more aware how gravely the erosion has set in among English communities. Greater London itself seems to have many areas where there is no sense of belonging to a community at all. Current economic forces, rehousing schemes, and the lack of any tangible boundary between one suburb and another doubtless all contribute to this, as does the fact that a large proportion of the population in Greater London is not from London at all, but from other parts of the British Isles. I kept on meeting young people who had drifted into London from one of the Northern cities, and the obvious inference of this is that families in those places are increasingly being divided by this internal migration.

But Man needs to live within stable communities, for only in this way can the basic shared beliefs and skills of human existence be transmitted. Increasingly, in the Modern World, highly expensive and artificial means are having to be sought to provide forms of community for particular purposes, as in the armed services, the hospitals, the caravan parks, the refuges for the homeless, and – in the last resort – the prisons. It can be said that the scale and expense of operating the many types of community of specialist function is itself a measure of the breakdown of community in the general sense. Such specialist communities isolate their participants from the mainstream of human existence, and their shared expertise in the occupation which has brought them together serves only to place their mental and conceptual framework at serious imbalance.

The breakdown of communities is matched by the breakdown of family groups. While in South London, I had personal contact with many individuals from broken homes and broken marriages, and saw something of the impressive array of highly trained personnel of the Social Service departments who have to work with the hurt participants in this widespread sort of distress. Through listening to people I heard a lot of the supposed reasons why family breakdown occurs, and among the reasons noted were inappropriate housing; the generation gap; incompatibility; stress at work or unemployment; an addiction problem; bad friends or influences: and many more. It is evident on a little reflection that though such answers do explain something, they each raise more questions than they answer, for the task of asking 'Why?', is only driven back one stage further.

A civilisation, or culture, if it is sufficiently stable and complete to be worthy of the name, has to operate as a <u>system</u>, a system in which, besides enjoying a certain autonomy removed from outside pressures and control, all the component groupings and activities interact with each other, so that the working of none of them can be taken in isolation from the rest.

If we find, on observing a modern city like London, that such basic human groupings as communities and families can no longer operate, then we are entitled to ask whether the Modern Civilisation, at least in the form which we know, is a viable and sustainable one at all. There does not appear to be a stable patterning of human relationship which ordinary people can identify with and make their own.

There are those for whom this is taken a stage further. It was clear to me, after meeting a number of young people in South London, that not only did they fail to fit into stable home and community environment – often because it was not effectively there – but also they formed *ad hoc* groups and identities of their own. Young people did not say to me that they were English: they told me they were 'Mods'; 'Gribos'; 'Skinheads'; 'Punks'; 'Bikies'; and so on. Moreover, I soon learnt that a number of gangs operated in the area where I was staying, and that gang violence was a frequent occurrence. It did not seem to me that the recently-arrived minority ethnic groups were much involved in such activity. This is what I would have expected, for usually they have a comparatively strong sense of community, of family solidarity, and retain a great deal of their ancestral culture. No, it was the young English people, even if they did not realise that they were English. And as far as I could see, they did not. They were unaware who they were. They had adopted false mob identities, for the urge to belong to something is very strong.

There is one whole area of communal life which I would have needed more time to observe accurately, and that was the persistence of customs surrounding the major events in the lives of individuals, such as Birth; Death; Entry into Adult Status; and Marriage, along with courtship.

Indeed, the picture that I did get within the time-span that I had was somewhat contradictory, which may indicate a period of transition. Births occurred within marriages, within informal man-woman relationships, and as a result of casual sexual liaison. It seemed to me that the available setting for courtship, which is a vital element in any human society, was very unsatisfactory, and the McDonalds Hamburger Bars and the local 'Discos' were scenes of recurrent violent and depraved behaviour, even though a very large number of the local young people met in those places.

In regard to Marriage, where it is clear that many are formally married while a substantial proportion are not, I came to realise that many rejected formal marriage as they saw it merely as 'A bit of paper'. The plain implication of this curious fact is that they had no awareness that Marriage, underneath the modern legal presentation of it, is a basic event within one's own society as a whole, wherein the two participants indicate their obligation to the people of their own civilisation and nationality to live together in a way sanctioned by the values, beliefs, and customs of that society. Instead, they saw Marriage Law as being on a par with The Factory Acts, or the laws relating to the use of seat belts.

It was in relation to Death that I observed the greatest readiness on the part of all, including the very young, to conform to a common received pattern of behaviour. The death of a teenager moved those of his age group very deeply, and their behaviour at the funeral was exemplary, as were also the sentiments that they voiced in all sincerity. I think that death always has this ability to recall deculturalised people to a common and sane mind, though in the mode of grief, while such people necessarily look to the older and established institutions of society at such a time for the want of any conceivable alternative.

But when we turn to what is a major element in archaic sorts of human society, the reception of young people into adult status, I find that there our Modern Civilisation is failing them almost completely.

It is a constant characteristic of young people that they should seek occasion to assay themselves in the skills of adulthood with its attendant dangers, and then seek to be admitted to adulthood by some tangible test which will win the recognition of society and in particular the recognition of their own age group.

In this respect, as in other cardinal aspects of human existence, it is the study of archaic tribal cultures that has provided Social Anthropology with its more reliable data, and this should not surprise us, for we are all descended from Mesolithic hunter-gatherers, and the most probable opinion is that Modern Man spent far, far longer in that phase than he has in any subsequent settled and technologically advanced sort. And what has been learnt from such data is that one of the most constant facts about human cultures and civilisations is that adolescents should undergo communally recognised and accepted experiences and ceremonies that signify in the eyes of the whole of that society, in the eyes of their own age-group, and not least in their own eyes, that they have acquired the status of adulthood.

The group behaviour of the young people that I observed in South London suggests strongly that they do not see acceptable models of adulthood among older people that they know, that they are actively seeking alternative models from whatsoever exotic or dubious source, and that they have ceased to be very concerned about their acceptance as adults by older people. Despairing of this, they concentrate on activities and attitudes that tend to secure acceptance among their own age group.

This severe and exaggerated age-group cleavage in fast-changing urban areas entails that little of worth can be culturally transmitted from the sources and founts of the civilisation of the people in question, and in the present instance that is the English people.

2. The estrangement of the English people from the land

Unquestionably, the Early English People, in the centuries that preceded the Norman Conquest, were a people who were intimately bound to the land, being in that respect like the Hebrews of the eighth century BC or the people of rural Southern Nigeria to this very day. Not only that, but they were well distributed over the land, as the evidence of modern place-names and of current archaeology strongly suggest. For six hundred years the Early English built up a highly successful and resilient civilisation of that sort before they were made slaves in their own land by the Norman imperial overlords. (I betray some prejudice here).

Currently, I know of no other people on the face of the Earth who have been so thoroughly dispossessed from the lands that their ancestors once lived on in some sector or another of the then labour-intensive rural economy. Perhaps Brazil would provide an interesting comparison. In the case of many a 'Third-World' country one reads of the sufferings of the rural population, often maltreated and exploited by the powerful classes in the respective capital city. But, nevertheless, they are still there. They are still on the land. The agricultural industry in rural England has largely phased out the human being as a factor in the rural-based economy, though seasonal workers are still grudgingly admitted, along with a new population of retired city-dwellers. This point applies to a large extent in Scotland as well, as I can personally testify.

After the earlier phase of the Industrial Revolution the English population was increasingly transferred into the conurbations, in order to serve the new sort of economy, which at that time was very much Empire-orientated. Since the Second World War, if not before, the population has also been expected to become much more mobile, both because the fortunes of individual industries became more uncertain, and also because the British economy as a whole became locked increasingly into that of *blocs* of trading partners over whose affairs – unlike those of the erstwhile Empire – Britain had little control. A third reason for this increased mobility was the much greater specialisation of skills required in the workforce, so that local employment for personnel of any particular grade became much more uncertain.

The conclusion to be drawn from all this is that 'Progress' has progressed so far that the English population is being shaped, moulded and remoulded by economic and commercial forces which are neither defined nor centred within the confines of our own nation and people. Increasingly our people have become enmeshed in the machinery of production, consumption, and administration that now bind us, no more to the land, but to an international network of trading partners who share the same patterns of commercial exploitation of an ever-developing technology. In short, the English People have become subservient to an alien economy which is not their own, and in which they have an increasingly uncertain share. In the meantime, through the means which are known as 'marketing', they are being taught to want things which they do not need and to forget what might remain of their indigenous culture in order to become simply a part of 'The West', with the consumption habits that go with it.

After what has just been asserted – with little danger of refutation, I think – it should be stressed that, within the traditional cultures which survived just long enough to be studied by the social anthropologists, each civilisation had its own kind of complete internal economy, integral to that particular culture, both complementing the other elements of that culture and also operating within and through them. In an ordinarily human way of life of a particular people, the economy is not only wholly within their total way of life but is also of a kind which is peculiarly their own.

This is not to deny that even in very ancient times there were forms of trade and a certain level of symbiosis among contiguous peoples, but the terms of such would have been by mutual agreement and would not have been at a level which would have called into question the very identity of any of the parties to such mutual activity. The complex linguistic map in what were till recently the preserves of the archaic cultures of mankind is sufficient evidence of this in itself.

3. The loss to the English people of their indigenous cultural traits

In every part of the world where a traditional way of life survives, the visitor is aware of an array of indicators of the local way of life, and he will note that the local people are communally proud of their skills in maintaining the tradition of these things.

Typically, a given people have their own music and dance, architecture, mode of dress and materials for the production of the same, culinary tradition, martial arts, and articles of craft ware – the latter properly having a function within the local economy. And in saying this, I do not just mean those places where the whole local scene has been geared to the consumption needs of the 'Western' tourist. For one thing, I have never had the money to be such a tourist. Rather, ask the Voluntary Service Overseas young people who work for a local wage in the deep Bush. They will tell of how the local people courteously introduce the resident foreigner to their local customs without a hint of ulterior motivation; merely the mutual desire to be neighbourly to a foreigner who, they assume, has been uprooted from a rich and varied way of life of his own. They will draw the foreigner who knows how to comport himself into an active participation in their indigenous pursuits, usually with a great deal of laughter initially! I have so often been thus privileged.

Then, what did I discover on my return to England? Briefly, this:

a. Popular music has been supplanted by a loud noise requiring electronic wizardry for its execution and transatlantic mass-marketing for its dissemination. Since I have travelled very widely and have heard dozens of kinds of indigenous music and have managed to like almost all and to enthuse about many, I think that my reaction is significant. I have reason to think that the English People of a thousand years ago had entrancing popular music. I read *The Battle of Maldon* in the original Anglo-Saxon and was reminded by a Scots businessman the other day that the whole thing must have been set to music. Only so, he explained, could they have remembered it. As for dancing, I was stunned to see that the young people, far from dancing, were simply watching young Afro-Caribbeans showing them how to dance.

b. The buildings that surround urban dwellers as they grow up have a powerful effect on their consciousness. I have to say that I know of no form of urban ugliness more acute than that which I observed in North Sutton while I was there. The old inner-city zones had an austere grimy humanness that persisted through their decay – as witness the popularity of 'Coronation Street' and 'The East Enders'. And I once worked in Newcastle East End. But there are now whole zones where the very form and texture of the buildings and their disposition among the urban freeways bespeaks the dominant importance of the process of quick money-making. An American colleague who worked with me at a language school in Milan told me that he could see no difference between Sutton and the standard American small town of the more nondescript sort. Well, we are all 'Westerners', aren't we?

c. There is no need to labour the point that in mode of dress the young people have nothing to distinguish them as being English. Even where the more outrageous of the young people set the trend in mode of attire, it is simply in a new variant of the general 'Western' way.

d. As for culinary tradition, English people now go to an Ethnic Restaurant if they want to go out for a meal. Left to themselves, they simply wander round supermarkets and pick convenience foods off the shelf to heat up later. The Scots, I am pleased to discover, retain their indigenous culinary forms, and in the relatively severe climate of Aberdeenshire I can be thankful that this is so. Without haggis, tatties and neaps, it is doubtful whether this piece could have been written. But in a local High Street in South London one can take the choice of an Indian Restaurant, a Chinese Restaurant, an Italian Trattoria, and a Greek Taverna – where is the English Restaurant? There is none.

e. Martial Arts. The very phrase now seems evocative of finely conceived traditions of combat from the far Orient, emanating from the disciplines of a centuries-old exotic spirituality. But have the English totally forgotten that they are descended from one of the great and renowned warrior peoples of ancient history? Are they wholly unaware of the heroic deeds of those who fought with Oswald, Alfred, Harold

Godwinesson and a host more? Do they know nothing of the way in which the English dispossessed the Ancient Britons who had grown supine under the refinements of the late Roman Empire? Are they without knowledge of the manner in which the English alone withstood the might of the Vikings under Alfred, and at Maldon, and, more tragically in view of what was to follow, at Stamford Bridge?

Indeed, the very name, *Saxon*, signifies *knife-warrior*. Recently an example of an Old English 'Seax' was on display in the British Museum, along with its inscription in the original native English script which, like the Irish Ogam, was later to be displaced by the Insular variant of the Roman Script.

The difference with the Irish and the Scots is that the awareness of their early skills and exploits is still very much with them. Nobody who knew the Early English people would ever suppose that their descendants would ask the folk from the Orient to show them how to fight.

In view of what I have just enumerated I am glad to observe that there is, in certain quarters, a renewal of ancient crafts and skills, but this is usually associated with fairly intellectual people who are themselves questioning the Modern Civilisation under the influence of the Ecological Movement.

4. The decay in the use of language

Now, there is abroad a strongly relativist school of thought on the subject of language. Those of this persuasion will argue that there are no norms in linguistic usage. "English is just how she is spoke", they will say.

In contrast, I take a more anthropological view. I believe that a language, belonging, as it usually does to a particular people, normally reflects their civilisation as a whole, just as it is the medium of some of its most important expressions. Since a healthy civilisation has a certain stability which will resist sudden and violent change, so too, the concomitant language will tend strongly at any given time to show norms of usage which can be demonstrated without falling into extremes of pedantry or of artificial ossification.

There is sound evidence for this. Some European societies had populations whose way of life changed relatively little over very many centuries, and such change as there was occurred slowly and without the serious socio-economic upheavals to which England especially has been subject. An example is Lithuania, whose language is an extremely archaic representative

41

of the Indo-European group, and of great complexity. In contrast, we know that Greek underwent serious changes in the wake of Alexander's conquests, that the stormy history of the Late Roman Empire was accompanied by the rise of Late Vulgar Latin and its subsequent shattering into mutually unintelligible Romance dialects.

The English Language began as the extreme north-western form of the Germanic group, and became Anglo-Saxon (Old English) subsequent to settlement in the main part of Britain. Though some Northern dialects became transmuted by infusion of Norse through the Vikings, West Saxon came to occupy the place of standard form, and the bulk of what has come down to us has reached us in that standard.

But English underwent two major transmutations, the transition from Old to Middle English in the wake of the Norman Conquest, and the change from Middle to Early Modern English seemingly in the period following the Wars of the Roses. In both cases, the linguistic confusion settled down into a new pattern which was capable of being moulded by a Chaucer or a Shakespeare into an artistic and literary medium in its own right.

But we must no longer be sure that such can happen again. Strong reasons can be adduced to support the view that the English language is in danger of decay, degradation, and disintegration. I will make these points:-

a. For well-known reasons, the English language has an unparalleled dissemination in the Modern World, and is widely used by a number of countries that have no special interest in preserving a standard close to the territorially English original. Nigeria, India, and the Caribbean peoples are examples which come to mind.

b. Since English is used elsewhere not only as a first language but in many more places as a second tongue, and has thus become a de facto international language, it follows that the English People have no distinctive current language of their own. This startling point deserves emphasis. The English no longer have a language which they can call peculiarly theirs.

c. In particular, the English People now spend a lot of their time in the evenings and at weekends listening to television programmes in American dialects, while it seems to be *de rigueur* for 'Pop' musicians to emulate the intonations and grammatical traits of the bad areas of Nashville, Tennessee.

d. The population of Greater London is now a large proportion of the whole population of England, and through the television the London dialects, which now diverge sharply from the standard, have a powerful influence over the whole of Britain, along with the American programmes already mentioned. This tends towards the suppression of the English dialects, which are very archaic in origin and preserve much of the original heritage from pre-Norman times. They also tend strongly to maintain the phonetic equilibrium of the English language, but only while they survive.

e. There is a marked deterioration in the quality of English as presented in the newspapers and on the television. Even the quality newspapers make amazing grammatical errors and spelling mistakes. On the television the newscasters, and in particular many of the male ones, have a phonetic distortion which I can only describe as 'quacking', and which I now hear commonly in the streets of South London.

f. In those same streets, I began to encounter what I believe is a new phenomenon for the human race. There is clear evidence of a lack or loss of basic competence in the spoken form of the mother tongue. I met young people who were literally incapable of putting into words any matter about which they felt deeply but which they were not accustomed to express in the spoken form. It has always been recognised that many people do not know the standard form of their language but only their regional dialect. It has always been true that many individuals fail to learn to read and write. That people should be unable to attain to competence even in the spoken form of their own dialect is, I would urge, a new and dangerous matter to investigate. Human beings can, under modern conditions, even lose the power of speech in part.

g. As a compensation, it seems, for this basic linguistic impoverishment, there is now a widespread practice in urban areas, for almost every spoken sentence to be reinforced by obscene expletives with a connotation of sexual violence. I can only say that I have travelled widely and have found that to be true only in one other place. That was Wyndham, Western Australia, where I was confronted with the very special case of the poor depraved Aborigines whose way of life had been so disrupted and overlaid with chronic alcoholism. No doubt they had picked up the words from the worst kind of European cattlemen.

43

There is no exaggeration on this issue. I had only to walk along Sutton High Street at any hour of the day or week, and I could be sure of hearing this filthy, degraded form of London dialect most of the time, along with the newer phonetic distortions and the sexually violent expletives. In the big industrial city of Milan and in Benin City, Nigeria, I came across no such thing.

What can be the meaning of all this? I believe that we have to bear in mind that the Human Race, in entering on the seemingly unprecedented experiment of the Modern Civilisation, has also subjected the human power of speech to tests which it has never previously had to undergo. It would be the height of complacency to assume, under current conditions, that the English Language can look after itself. I believe that what is happening to the English Language is already a clear indicator of the deculturalisation of which I speak, and that the sciences of linguistics and semantics must be drawn upon along with social anthropology.

5. The shattering and dissolution of the basic conceptual field

Every human civilisation and culture has deep roots, and the most persistent element in any of such will be a set of basic concepts, held in the minds of the people concerned, and transmitted and shared by them over many generations. For any such people, these basic concepts will constitute their own peculiar way of seeing the world in which they live, and will include their underlying system of values – what they believe to be right and wrong, important and unimportant, revered or despised.

I suppose that any gardener knows that when a plant withers, it is likely that something is gnawing at the roots, and this analogy should lead us to ask what are the roots of the civilisation and culture of the English People.

In the archaic tribal cultures, it was a vital aspect of all of them, despite their amazing diversity on so many matters, that they should have a recognised manner of imparting the wisdom, lore, and myths, as received from their ancestors from time immemorial, to each successive group of candidates for adulthood. That the mechanism of transmission is missing I have already pointed out, but are there now any elements within reach to transmit?

Even in their present condition, the Australian Aborigines often pointed out to me that they had their 'Law'. Their particular use of the English word was significant, for it would have corresponded closely to the Old

English Æ and to Norse equivalents. They were speaking of Sacral Law, which is by nature unchanging and derived from a primal, unimpeachable source. Originally, the English had a sacred mythology of the Heathen sort – using the word 'heathen' in its original sense of indigenous culturally derived religion – and this they shared with the Vikings and other Germanic tribal peoples. The Celtic peoples would have had a very similar system in principle. But like the Irish, and in large measure through the Irish, the English exchanged the Heathen religion, with its rich mythology, for the primitive Catholicism of the First Millennium. The story of how King Edwin and his counsellors considered the merits of the New Faith is one of the gems of English literature, as it has reached us in the medium of the Anglo-Saxon language.

It can be argued, and in theological circles I will argue, that the Christianity of the First Millennium was much more balanced and whole than it subsequently became from the Twelfth Century onwards. While the English, after a lot of initial resistance, finally adopted the Christian Faith wholeheartedly, they found that they could at the same time retain substantially what was good and noble from the value system and conceptual field of the Old Religion and mythology, for it had had much in it that was a real *praeparatio evangelii*. That this is so is shown by literary gems such a *The Dream of the Rood* where the Christian theme has a distinctly Northern and Germanic presentation, and in *The Battle of Maldon*, where a brilliant exposition of the ancient Germanic heroic warrior ideal is set forth in what had long been a Christian context.

What can supply this 'Sacral Law' now, in our own time? The Americans may well evoke 'The American Dream' and 'The Frontier Spirit', but that is theirs, and not ours. I submit that we must return to the original sources of our culture and reconsider the six hundred years of our known history before the Norman Conquest and see what we can draw from it.

As far as the Church is concerned in our own time, I will say this. These are times when the Church is repairing the damage done over many centuries. I believe that the Christian Church is recovering afresh the insights and springs of spirituality which she knew in early times. The old division between Catholic and Protestant will be healed, and the even more ancient one between Catholic and Eastern Orthodox, as well as between the latter and the ancient Oriental Rites.

45

This damage was almost certainly caused by the entanglement of the Church within the cultural and economic distortions of the age in which the harm was done. The Church, as Custodian and Repository of the Divine Law, must in principle and in Spirit remain detached from the World in which nevertheless she has to witness and to live at any given time.

We are right to tolerate and to respect alien religions in so far as they are integral to the way of life of this or that minority ethnic group. We are totally wrong, however, to embrace a spiritual relativism which argues that all religions are equal and equally unimportant. For the English People desperately need the Christian Faith which their ancestors once cleaved to without question. There is no escape from this issue. The question of what are the basic values and beliefs of any particular people is inescapably a religious one. I am prepared to listen to an argument that the Christian Religion is the wrong one for The English now – though I would vigorously counter such a suggestion – but I will not listen to any suggestion that no religion is needed, for human beings are unable to live without a shared set of precepts and beliefs which they unquestionably hold in common. Where else can they obtain such a thing, if not from a religion, whether it be indigenous or from elsewhere?

It is for this reason that the question of true religion is of concern to the Government of a particular people. The English are no exception. In practice, the Monarch continues to be crowned with the solemnities of the Church just as in the days of Athelstan or Egbert, and modern governments continue to be alarmed when the zeal of an alien cult claims large numbers of adherents from among our young people. And rightly so, for an alien cult may well have an alien value system. The Church may know of additional reasons. King Alfred knew how important the matter was.

Unless and until it can be demonstrated that the English People retain the option of returning to the noble and heroic ideals of the warriors and saints that stud the pages of our early history, the danger remains that young English people will turn in increasing numbers to exotic and oriental sources for their spiritual inspiration, while those who do not will sink into the depression of meaningless materialism, relieved only by the drug scene, or by whatever form of escapism lies to hand.

Quite apart from the transmission of fundamental beliefs and values from Early English times, we may well ask how much reaches the modern English population about the events and personages of Early English history. I once hitched a lift from a truck driver who turned out to be a Kerry man of dubious sobriety. However, he was able to debate with me the importance of the Battle of Clontarf at which Briain Boru is said to have inflicted a defeat on the Vikings. " 'Twas a mere skirmish", he opined. In the same way, ordinary working people in Northern Italy can speak at length on the cultural treasures of their own region, while knowing enough to depreciate those of other regions! I would like to think that young English people had at least the option of learning about the skills, the language, the history, and the social organisation of the Early English People. I wonder what young English People are being taught in, say, the Inner London Education Authority area. Is not the primary and fundamental thing in education the manner in which children are told who they are? If they are denied that, or if, worse still, they are seriously misinformed on this matter, then it is not too much to say that very grave harm is being done to those children.

6 The progressive loss of awareness of identity among the English people

My experience in England in 1984 and 1985 leads me to state that many English people are by now unaware who they are. This is deculturalisation taken to an extreme in one direction. I met a young man on an archaeological dig, under the 'Community Programme'. The conversation happened to turn to the topic of peoples and their characteristics. "The Welsh, the're the real English, aren't they?", was the supposition of this young man.

Many reasons are forthcoming for this erosion of the sense of identity among the English People. Ever-increasing mobility in response to changes in the economic climate and world markets. The moulding effect of urban living as opposed to the rural way of life which most of our ancestors enjoyed or endured until fairly recent times. The very heavy 'Class' divisions in English society, such that for many the sense of belonging to a particular social-economic class outweighs the sense of belonging to a 'People'. Then there is the growth of the international 'Meritocracy', through which many feel much more intensely than any other affiliation the sense of membership of a particular achievement group, such as the pilots of international flights and persons in top management.

Many other reasons connected with the loss of salient cultural traits and ignorance of cultural roots and origins have already been noted.

Now, however, it is becoming clear that this vagueness about who they are on the part of the English is leading to the appearance of false and substitute identities. This is even more serious.

It has long been clear that many deculturalised young people have been forming sub-cults, each having its distinct traits of dress and 'pop' musical predilections, as well as a readiness to show violence to others of a different group persuasion. The misuse of the tradition of football fan clubs is an aspect of all this.

But in other ways, the gradual assumption of false identities of a substitute nature pervades the whole population. In journalism and on the broadcast media we read and hear 'We in The West ...'; The West must ...'; 'You Westerners ...'; 'Western Culture is responsible for ...'; and so on. How long have we been 'Westerners'? When I was very young The West was The United States of America. I do not think of myself as a 'Westerner'. The so-called 'Western' culture is not our original one at all. It is something that has been done to us. If anything, I am a 'Northerner'.

And apparently there are no Englishmen overseas. In the newspapers we read 'Britons resident in ...'; 'Five Britons are being held hostage ...'; and so on. Scotsmen are far more likely to be recognised for what they are, since they are likely to insist on it. Britain is a Union of distinct peoples.

And now a much graver aspect of this destruction of identity must be mentioned, for the implications of it are very grave indeed. Subsequent to my arrival in England early in 1984 I was dismayed, and indeed horrified, to discover that in the newspapers and on the television there had grown up in my absence a widespread practice of referring to my fellow countrymen – if they were not obviously of one of the darker-complexioned minority ethnic groups – as 'Whites'; or 'UK Whites'.

The clear inference is that the journalists do not know what else to call them, or if they do, then they do not think that it is important. In contrast, I regard this usage as deeply offensive. I, personally, will never allow myself to be referred to as a 'UK White', but wish to be known as an Englishman, as my forefathers have been for countless generations. I do not wish to be redefined.

At this stage, although I have allowed my personal feelings to be known, that is not what is important. There are a good many objective reasons why the White terminology must not be allowed, for the implications are serious.

a. The use of the term White encourages the fracture of society along the lines of incidental racial characteristics, instead of allowing people to be grouped together according to their cultural integrity and affiliation.

b. Because of recent history in the USA and the extensive news coverage given to the tragic events that took place in the Republic of South Africa, there is a very real danger that foreign usage and connotations may permeate the English population and other ethnic groups in Britain in connection with the word 'White' used in this way.

c. The term 'White' is commonly used in an offensive, pejorative way, especially in certain kinds of political journalism where one finds such expressions as 'White attitudes'; 'White, Anglo-Saxon Protestant'; 'White power groups', and the like. Aware as I am that those to whom this piece is addressed will regard these expressions as nonsensical, I hope nevertheless that they will still see that in current parlance among ordinary people they can become dangerous as well as offensive, as they involve a serious abuse of language in common use.

d. The term 'White' used in this way is, in any case, meaningless on examination, for North African Berbers (whom I once taught in a language institute) are as pallid-skinned as Europeans. So are the Turkic peoples and the populations of Eastern Asia.

e. Most serious of all, however, is the implication of this false usage that the terms 'English' and 'Englishman' are obsolete. I strongly deny this implication. In England, a territory which the English tribes conquered and occupied with exceptional thoroughness in the fifth and sixth centuries, and from which they have never been displaced by any subsequent invasion, it should be regarded as a matter of historical justice that any resident British citizen in the territory known as England should be regarded as English unless there is good reason to suppose otherwise.

There is no need, then, to call people 'Whites'. We should usually be able to assume that any British citizen we see in England is English. Should he be a Scotsman; a British Sikh; an Afro-Caribbean of British nationality; a Pole; or a member of the British Chinese community, then either he will be able to say so, or else it will be amply clear through a series of cultural and linguistic markers that show us what he really is.

On this very matter I wrote to a number of organisations that act in a 'watchdog' capacity with regard to racially discriminatory or racially offensive practices. Either it was not directly their concern, or else I received a mildly polite reply.

Then, I wrote to the Director General of the BBC because of the persistent use of the 'White' terminology on television programmes. Receiving a first reply which suggested that I had not been understood, I wrote a much fuller second letter. To this second letter I received the truly astonishing reply that they were amazed that I should continue to believe that there was now a particular people called 'The English'.

In other words, in the official view of the British Broadcasting Corporation, a body which helps more than any other institution to mould public opinion, the main people that they serve simply does not exist!

This same view I also heard expressed by a member of Sinn Fein, but that it should also be official BBC doctrine puts an entirely different complexion on the matter.

I understand that it is now fashionable in many quarters to play down the existence of the English People in this way. The argument employed is a double one. They assert, first of all, that the original English invasion of Britain in the late fifth century was numerically only small, though they admittedly succeeded in establishing a political and cultural ascendancy. The second part of the argument is to the effect that so many people of many kinds have settled in England through the subsequent centuries, that any supposed English ancestry can only be a very minor element. It is not difficult to counter these arguments.

First, with the Anglo-Saxon scholar Dorothy Whitelock (*The Beginnings of English Society*, Penguin 1952) I would argue that the Anglo-Saxon language itself demonstrates that the English settlement of the main part of Britain must have been extremely thorough and ruthless. Very, very few words from the old British language survive in it. The distribution of Anglo-Saxon place names, still extant or otherwise, likewise argues for a very thorough occupation. And the English culture that persisted for six hundred years before the Norman Conquest, as demonstrated in the literary relics, is a Germanic culture, as we would expect of the English.

Secondly, no subsequent invasion succeeded in displacing the English people. In the special case of The Vikings, we are considering a people who were in any case very closely related to the English indeed, with a nearly identical culture. The main difference was that they had retained the Heathen Religion longer. After their defeat at the hands of Alfred, they gradually became assimilated to the English if they had already settled in England.

True, the Norman Invasion was a disaster for the English, but it is important to note what the Normans did not do. They did not displace the English population. They even failed to impose their curious dialect of French on the English, though the development of the English Language was violently distorted at the time. In any case, they, too, were a Germanic people who had – unlike the English of that time – been deculturalised.

We are then told that hordes of other settlers have come to England from every quarter. On this argument, the pallid-faced people who now inhabit England are descended for the most part from Huguenot refugees, Slavic Jews escaping from pogroms, and Chinese laundrymen! This shows a massive lack of sense of proportion. Without denying that such people have joined the English through the centuries, we have simply to ask what happened to the English population. There was no massacre, no enforced migration, and the inference is that for a modern Englishman it is most reasonable to suppose that his ancestry is English for the most part. What else can we call ourselves?

It must be carefully observed, at this point, that nothing more is being claimed than that for the modern English the Anglo-Saxon element is by far the most significant one in their ancestry. No spurious claim of supposed 'racial purity' is being put forward. No more is being claimed, but also, let it be understood, no less than this. There is no other reasonable basis for our conscious identity as a people.

It may be thought that rather a lot is being made of this issue, but I have good reason to think otherwise. While I was in Australia, I learnt that only a quarter of a century ago, the Australian Government policy towards the Aboriginal People was that of assimilation. It was hoped, and not from base motives, that the Aboriginal People would simply be absorbed by the European-originated population and thus disappear off the map as a distinct people. In the event, the Australian Aborigines refused to be assimilated, and even showed that they would prefer physical destruction to such a fate. An English writer on ethnic affairs whom I met described such a policy of assimilation as 'Ethnocide'. As distinct from genocide, ethnocide does not involve the physical annihilation of individual human beings, but it does entail the destruction of a particular people, so that as a people they no longer exist.

Now that I am back in the United Kingdom, and have had time to see the extent of the deculturalisation of the English People, I now believe that 'ethnocide', with the sense just alluded to, is a fate that could befall the English. What helps to make the danger so great is the immense influence of a very centralised sort that the broadcast media and education curricula have over the minds of the very young and impressionable.

What am I to say when I hear that English children are told that they are just 'Whites' who have no culture of their own except the 'Western Way of Life', and who therefore will do well to learn from the profound diversity of cultural treasures of the non-European ethnic groups?

What can I say when it is propounded on the television and in political journals that the English People no longer exist, as so much has happened since the year 1066?

But the greatest danger lies not in such things but in the misuse of individual words. A word can contain a much more profound lie than a whole paragraph: the science of semantics teaches us that. The use of such words as 'White' and 'Western' is already extremely dangerous as a sort of semantic cuckoo-in-the-nest leaving no room for 'English' in anyone's consciousness.

Let this be said: if the English People no longer exist, as some assert with glee, then what is to be done with the many millions of mainly pallid-complexioned people, in the territory of England, who have no other identity or origin at all, if not an English one? It cannot be stressed too strongly that if they are denied any identity or culture, then they will become progressively ungovernable, and increasingly prone to degradation, addictions, and violence of every sort. Should anyone doubt this, then let him inquire into the present condition of the city fringe-dwelling remnants of the Southern Aboriginal tribes in Australia. They didn't die out. Only their culture died out, and they are still there; a massive headache for the State Governments in Australia.

7. The Relationship between the English and other peoples and ethnic groups in the United Kingdom

In view of the manner in which I have just expressed myself in respect of my own people and my fears concerning them, what I have to say next may be something of a surprise. Briefly, the fact that I am 'for' The English does not mean that I am 'against' all the others.

Concerning The Scottish People, who have always had to live next door to The English, I need say very little, for they are fully capable of speaking for themselves. I am aware, now that I find myself here in Aberdeenshire, that the Scots are anxious about what is happening to the English. It is here, in Scotland, that I am referred to as an Englishman in a way that would never happen in London. Much of what I have said about English identity and culture could be transferred to the Scottish situation, with the proviso that the Scots, while under pressure from the Modern Civilisation, show no immediate danger of deculturalisation as I have discussed that term. Or is this totally true? While in London I did learn that a very large number of young Scots are drifting into London, hoping to find work and a place to live. And the young Morayshire lad who works with me in the YTS scheme tells me very disquieting things about Aberdeen. I can also say that many Scots feel disquiet about the terms of the 1707 Union of the two parliaments.

As an Englishman staying in a Scottish Burgh, I am astonished at the persistence of a distinct Scottish Culture which shows itself at many levels. And I am reassured by this. I believe that the Scots are very displeased about all the things which collectively I have labelled 'deculturalisation' among the English, and I suspect that in any mass movement on the part of the English to rediscover themselves as a people, they will have the encouragement and understanding of the Scots.

I refrain from speaking of the Welsh and Cornish at this point without having opportunity to live among them.

It is at this point that I will discuss the relationships between the English and the newly-arrived ethnic minorities.

Honesty compels me to say at the outset that I feel that the post-war influx of culturally contrasting ethnic groups happened over the heads of ordinary English people, but as an English factory hand said to me, "Well, they're here now; we've got to accept that." But grudgingly? It need not be so, to my mind. Let us admit, though, that the whole thing took place with the encouragement of Big Business and global market forces. It might be more to the point, now, to ask what were the motives of the individual men and women who decided to come to England from very distant parts of the Commonwealth. And that I do not pretend to know. At a guess, I should suppose that it was often a spirit of adventure, since my own people have often been motivated in that way.

What I have already said about human culture and civilisation, and the dire need of the English People to recover their cultural integrity, has clear implications here.

Double standards must be avoided in this discussion at all costs, and what I have asserted to be true of the English as regards their basic needs is paralleled by the needs of the minority ethnic groups, as I understand them. I believe that it would be a disaster for them, too, to lose their indigenous culture and identity in exchange for participation in that highly artificial phenomenon called 'The West'. Is that what they really want? I think it highly unlikely, though I must not presume to speak on their behalf.

I believe that persons from the minority ethnic groups, living in England with British nationality, should have a clear choice. This would be:

Complete assimilation to the English People, whose culture, way of thinking and antecedents they would then be able to regard as their own. (This would correspond to the Anglo-Saxon concept of *giesling*.)

The obverse of this would be that such a person would have to be whole-hearted in his acquired English identity by adoption, and would not then be expected to turn round and say, "Ah, but we Yoruba " or the like. No one can ride two horses at the same time. And no one can row up two rivers simultaneously.

The other choice would be to continue to belong to one's own ancestral people, and in particular, to that section of them that had British nationality. This is largely what has happened, in fact. So it is that we have British-Chinese; British-Vietnamese; British-Sikhs; British-Bengalis; British-Caribbeans; and so forth.

So what is the problem? In principle, I do not think that there is any problem except what I have already been discussing – the deculturalisation of the English People. The presence of the minority ethnic groups within England affects this issue in more than one way. I will enumerate:

a. The first choice, that of assimilation, is not effectively open to most persons of the minority ethnic groups, since the English cultural base has become so weakened that they are unable to perceive an English culture as distinct from what they see as 'The West'. Any assimilation, then, that does take place is to 'The West', so that they become 'Westerners'. It is not then surprising if their children find this as unpleasing a prospect as do their English counterparts.

b. Since the English are the majority ethnic group, the symptoms of deculturalisation are liable to spread from the English to the youth of the minority ethnic groups, as we have already seen in some of the Inner City areas. This, I understand, affects the people of Caribbean extraction more urgently, as their family bonds are less formal than, say, those from traditionally Muslim countries. Their history would explain this.

c. The term 'English' has become so vague in current usage, that many people of the minority ethnic groups claim to be 'English' on the grounds that they have a British passport, or because they were born in England. I object to this in the strongest possible terms. British they are, since they are citizens of the same State in the modern sense, but English they are not.

I have already explained that I should hope that individual members of minority ethnic groups should be free to become English by adoption and preference, but to claim to be 'English' on the grounds just mentioned, while continuing to regard themselves as 'Rastafarians'; 'Sikhs'; 'Estonians' or the like, is to empty the word 'English' of any meaning. Effectively, that is to deny to English people any identity of their own.

To take one example. On the way back from Australia, I paid a visit to some Scottish friends then working in Malaysia. There, I met the indigenous Malays, the Chinese of Malaysian nationality, and the Indians of Malaysian nationality. They were all Malaysians – citizens of the state of Malaysia, but the Malays were and are a distinct people. The Chinese do not become Malays simply because they are born in Malaysia, nor do the Indians become Malays, for that reason. There, too, three distinct ethnic groups share the same nationality, but only one of them is the indigenous, and still the majority one. (I do not imply that no other ethnic group exists there). No Malay would he satisfied at being called a 'Pale Brown'.

Although I am upset by this abuse and devaluation of the word 'English' I am not thereby blaming the minority ethnic groups for this. It has not been made plain to them that there is, in fact, as distinct people called 'The English', having their own peculiar origins and cultural base.

d. I could modify what I said previously about the base of the population being properly regarded as English in one important respect. There is one ethnic group which has entered England in very large numbers over the last two hundred years, and whose relationship with the English, although close and cordial in Anglo-Saxon times, has since been strained. I refer, of course, to the Irish.

There must be a very large element intermingled with the English population who are still quite conscious that they are wholly or largely of Irish extraction. It occurs to me that, unless adoption and participation within the English community remains something attractive and culturally significant, large numbers of these people may eventually decide to revert to being Irish. When we add to that the probability that significant numbers of such families still have difficult and disorderly young people, we have to bear in mind the possibility of a dangerous form of internal disaffection, fed by and linked to well known groups within Ireland itself.

Indeed, if one is to judge from the propaganda that reaches us from the persons who style themselves 'Provisional IRA', they are unaware of the continued existence of the English and Scottish peoples. It would appear that they perceive what they call 'Brits'. I think it highly probable that there is, within the Irish population, a great deal of bitterness at the disruptive impact of the Modern Civilisation upon their national way of life and culture. In other words, the Irish tend to understand the threat of deculturalisation, and tend to want to fight against it. However, deculturalisation and the Modern Civilisation are very intangible, nebulous enemies, and because of this, an element within the Irish population uses ample historical excuses for transferring the aforesaid bitterness to an enemy that they can see. Hence the bitterness directed against the 'Brits'.

Here, then, is another reason why the English, especially, should make plain their continued existence as a people, and should make it clear that they are themselves in large measure victims of the Modern Civilisation and the cultural disruption that it has brought in its train. Do the Irish see anything other than wholly 'westernised' Brits?

e. In certain respects, there is an imbalance between the English and the minority ethnic groups, to the disadvantage of the former. This arises from the cultural disruption already discussed concerning the English, in strong contrast with the high degree of cultural integrity among the minority ethnic groups. I am not thinking here primarily of cultural traits such as folk music, but even more of the fundamental matter of family structure and traditions concerning the regulation of basic human relationships. Here the minority ethnic groups have a strong advantage at once, though the way in which this advantage operates varies from one people to another. And what must be made crystal clear at this point is that in this, the minority ethnic groups are behaving normally. It is the English who are in the abnormal position, for it is they who hove suffered the severe cultural disruption even in the most basic and fundamental matters of our common human existence.

In modern conditions, the various forms of the clan and the extended family provide a form of security, financial stability, and shared expertise, that cannot but be used. It is admittedly difficult to make this point because we are still haunted by the hideous memory of anti-Semitism from early in the century. The Jews did have this particular advantage, just like any other traditionally-minded People with strong cultural cohesion, though the hatred that was directed against them had other roots as well. The case of the Igbo tribe in the Nigerian Civil War is another instructive example. It is right and normal that people of any ethnic group should use their cultural integrity and cohesiveness to further their well-being, but this sort of group behaviour does necessitate a careful watch on the balance of advantage between the ethnic groups.

It should go without saying that the Early English, like all the Germanic Tribal peoples, had very strong family traditions, and the Modern English would do well to study what they were. The sources are still there. On the other hand, the modern way of life in the English cities must threaten to dissolve the fabric of social cohesiveness among the minority ethnic groups as well, and this is a prospect which must be unwelcome to all.

f. Too often, while I was in South London recently, I read of what were described and understood as racist attacks on families of Asiatic origin. Such events as these are abhorrent to sane and thinking people of any acceptable human tradition. These attacks were usually said to have been perpetrated by 'white people', or 'white youths'.

There is no need to attempt to deny this. I think that this is probably correct. But what can be done about it? 'Whites', as such, cannot take responsibility for anything. There is no conceivable moral stance or sense of a common self-respect involved in being a 'white youth'. But we do well to see that such behaviour has roots which must be dealt with at that level.

The long-term answer, then, is to encourage young English people – for that is probably who these 'white youths' are without even realising it – to see themselves as English, and thus as heirs of an extremely ancient and honourable cultural tradition of which they can be proud, while at the same time becoming open to the noble beliefs and code of behaviour which would preclude racism. What would Alfred the Great or Bishop Wulfstan have said of racist attacks?

For 'racism', especially in its violent phase, is an expression of envy, one of the most destructive of Man's attitudes of mind and spirit. Those who rediscover their identity and cultural integrity are no longer tempted to envy.

And now I will speak more personally about deculturalisation. On my return to England I was told roundly, "You must now remember that you belong to a multi-racial society".

I will reply to that, equally roundly, "I do not want to belong to a multi-racial society, and do not consider myself as so belonging. Yes, I am a citizen of a multi-ethnic state, but I belong to the English People. To my fellow citizens who are Sikhs, Afro-Caribbeans, and others I say that if any of them want to put behind them their original cultural traditions and become English by assimilation then I, for one, will welcome them. If they prefer to remain Sikhs and Afro-Caribbeans of British nationality, then I gladly accept my obligation and privilege to live alongside them in mutual harmony and respect, conscious that there are real advantages in having a contrast of cultures within the one territory."

Those who speak of a 'multi-racial society', and that not from any base motive as I can personally testify, mean something very different from the 'multi-ethnic state' which the United Kingdom and Malaysia, among others, truly are. What they mean is a new sort of society in which everyone conveniently puts behind him or herself any awkward reservations about history and indigenous culture, in order to merge into a single people bound together by all the supposedly wonderful things that we share in the Modern Civilisation. In short, we are all to become 'Westerners', and to be content with that.

If the Modern Civilisation were such a wonderful thing, I would at least see something to be put in favour of such a notion, but very powerful and extensive arguments can be adduced to the effect that it is not at all a wonderful thing, but the very reverse. (These arguments can only be given in the form of a book, and I have been writing one such.) People can hardly be expected to forget their origin and identity in favour of a new-found unity on the basis of a New Civilisation unless that new civilisation is at least something desirable. The English, who along with The Scots, have had to live with the Industrial Revolution and its consequences for longer than anyone else, have no reason to be satisfied with the so-called 'Western' civilisation as a basis for their common existence.

Moreover, there is a very unpleasant double standard involved in this notion of 'multi-racial society' as I hear it being propounded.

On the one hand, every allowance is made, and rightly so in my view, for those members of the British minority ethnic groups who wish to put into practice their cultural tradition in this new British context. Understandably, they want facilities for the practice of their religion and for the transmission of their own language. Adjustments are expected of them in certain matters such as the manner in which beasts are to be slaughtered for cultic purposes. And in the United Kingdom I believe that the minority ethnic groups have a very real freedom to live in their own manner as distinct peoples under the umbrella of the laws of The Realm.

On the other hand, when one such as myself expresses a like desire to live as an Englishman, with the whole range of cultural characteristics and consciousness of a particular origin and way of thinking that such implies, then he finds he is countered by comments about Hitler and the Third Reich, or accusations of racism, or a bewilderment that he should still believe in the existence of the English People. He may even find himself linked in the mind of the hearer with shady groups of 'heavies' in 'skinhead' attire who are said to intimidate unfortunate Asiatics. (Such do exist, I believe).

Yes it is a double standard. And the people who thus look askance at one who would assert his Englishness, quite apart from making every allowance for British ethnic minorities, are ready to support the cause of peoples like the Kurds or Armenians and others whose continued existence as distinct peoples is an embarrassment to some modern centralist government of this or that political hue. As long as they are not English.

And to the members of the British minority ethnic groups themselves, I should want to say just this:

"Do you want to become just 'Westerners'? Do you want to live in a society where in the end people are called just 'Blacks' or 'Whites'?"

"Did you think I was a 'Westerner'? Well, please correct that impression." "It is to your advantage, too, that the English should recover their own civilisation, for you have chosen to live alongside them. People who have lost their own culture and who have nothing worthwhile to put in its place are very unpleasant to live with." "It is my hope that individuals from your people should have the option of electing to become English and to be embraced by the English cultural tradition without ever being under any compulsion or even pressure to do so."

"I will not have it that the English way of life either is or was better than that of anyone else, while I hope that you will understand if I say that I believe that it was once as good as any."

And one last thing on this. Those whose business it is to delve into the cultural treasures of the traditional times find that there is much that peoples have in common all over the world. My own time spent among people in Southern Nigeria and Northern Australia especially, convinced me that what I had found there had a lot that reminded me of what I had heard and read about the Anglo-Saxons.

The inference of this is plain. Should the English succeed in recovering their cultural integrity on the basis of contact with what they once had, then they will be in a much better position to understand end respect the special characteristics of what may currently seem to them to be very alien patterns of existence.

It is surely deculturalisation that has opened the way to racist behaviour. And to implement a systematic denial that a particular people even exists is just about the worst force of racism that there is.

The cultural base of the English People
An adequate theoretical base
for the analysis of deculturalisation
and for seeking modes of reconstruction

At some length I have discussed the various modes, with the convenient term 'deculturalisation', in which the English People are threatened with the fragmentation and dissipation of their form of civilisation, and with loss of identity as a distinct people.

This must now be balanced by raising the question of what might be an adequate theoretical base for understanding and countering deculturalisation.

1. The study of civilisations and cultures

At this point I admit straightaway that I believe that the Government lacks the right sort of theoretical knowledge from the necessary disciplines of human studies. This would not be the first time that this has been so. In the earlier days of the Colonial Period, when the Colonial Office was having to exercise British Rule through the mediacy of traditional chieftains in regions like East Africa, there was at first a great deal of difficulty in understanding who were the persons with real power to wield, what sort of power it was, and how different sorts of power were distributed among different personages. This in itself was to beg the question as to whether the concept of 'power' as nineteenth century Britons understood the word was at all applicable among people and tribes with a very different way of life and thinking.

At the present time, I suspect that there is an underlying complication within the intellectual world itself. There would seem to be four main human disciplines of study which claim competence to examine a human culture or civilisation. These are:-

- Archaeology;
- History;
- Social Anthropology;
- Sociology.

Of these, Archaeology yields results which seem to supplement and extend what is found out by the historians and the Social Anthropologists. History examines a particular people or civilisation with reference to its successive phases, marked by particular events where necessary, in sequence on a time scale.

The difficulty lies in deciding what are the relative domains of Sociology and Social Anthropology, and the relationship between the two disciplines. This question, it seems to me, is of grave importance for the human race, and is not merely an academic quibble. It concerns what we chance to believe about the human race.

On one view, all the separate local histories and diverse traditional cultures of very many sorts have had a temporary existence which is now drawing to a close as they are being inexorably chased out by a coming new World Order based on High Technology; Vast Urban Complexes; Sophisticated Managerial and Communications Systems; and World-Wide Trade in Materials and in Knowledge and Ideas. This Modern Civilisation, which on this view is optimistically seen as destined to unite men and women everywhere, is thought to be undergoing its birth pangs.

On another, very different view, there is no such underlying concept of progress and irreversible change that we descry in the first one. The concept of 'Progress' is seen to be a temporary nineteenth century philosophical error. Civilisation and cultures are not seen on a scale of 'primitive' to 'advanced', and all human ways of life are seen to be of equal worth and to be held in the same esteem – be they archaic tribal hunter-gatherers or technologically sophisticated city dwellers – provided that each and all of them satisfy the basic norms without which a human culture cannot exist at all, or only at the cost of human misery, degradation, and damage to the Earth on which we live.

On this second view, too, the normal condition of the human race is that the Earth should be covered with a 'patch-work quilt' of mutually contrasting civilisations and cultures of widely differing characteristics. This is a principle of plurality of cultures, which I take to be a fundamental fact for the human race on Earth. It has to be said that the Modern Civilisation is threatening to destroy this plurality, without which I believe that Man cannot safely live on Earth.

Again, on this second view, the fact that the Modern Civilisation is technologically very clever does not of itself commend it, while this same civilisation is heavily criticised for its demographic imbalance, its divisiveness and instability, its organisational complexity, its wastefulness of natural resources such as soil, and its erosion of genuine human cultural traits, which it does little to foster and much to destroy.

Returning now to the vexed question about the relationship between the disciplines of Social Anthropology and Sociology.

Sociology is a vast science with very many departments, but I think that it suffers from a grave weakness in its basic pre-suppositions. Sociology leaves unanswered the question of cultural relativism. It is a human science which assumes that whatever phase of the Modern Civilisation it is operating within is to be taken as normal. Since the Modern Civilisation itself appears to be changing at an accelerating rate, this must call into question not only the hypotheses that are framed in Sociology, but also the methods of sociometry that are developed by social scientists living and working within a particular cultural milieu.

Moreover, the various branches of Sociology do indeed set great store by exact measurement and the application of the mathematics of statistics. This is not wrong in itself, but overlooks the fact that quantitative observation in human matters should be secondary to conceptual analysis – the meaning of observed human events, or the semantics of human behaviour, to put it another way. A pattern of human behaviour, as physically observed, may have one interpretation put on it within our Modern Civilisation, and yet what on the surface would appear to be the same behaviour might have a very different significance indeed in another civilisation, not least in the conscious minds of the participants. Sometimes, it is true, just such a cross-cultural consideration may lead us to look for a renewed similarity, by questioning whether we were right in the first place in our original interpretation of the observed behaviour within the Modern setting!

Now it is precisely the Science of Social Anthropology which sets out to confront the question of cultural relativism, and to search the boundaries of variability in the formation of human civilisations. In Social Anthropology, we are taught how to look for the semantic content of observed human behaviour, partly by becoming familiar with the indigenous language, and partly by seeing how the points of behaviour observed at one time fit into the way of life of the given people taken as a whole.

In Social Anthropology, we are given as in no other science save, in a special and more restricted way, that of Archaeology, the opportunity to consider such fundamental human questions as:-

- What traits, if any, can be found in all whole and independent human societies?

- What characteristics are found as absolutely indispensable in human civilisations?

- What happens when a civilisation is destabilised by the introduction of a new factor, such as the invention of gunpowder or a new philosophical idea?

- How resilient are human civilisations in the face of natural disasters and changes of climate?

- What sorts of human civilisation fit in best with the ecosystems of the Earth?

- Are there any ways of developing criteria for the relative evaluation of human cultures and civilisations?

The last question is an extremely difficult one to answer, but at least the Science of Social Anthropology gives us the methodology for finding the relevant data as a background to the question.

In short, I believe that Sociology should really be related to Social Anthropology as a sub-division of the latter, dealing specifically with the Modern Civilisation. But the conceptual bases of Sociology would then have to be re-examined.

But the main point that I wish to make, arising from the present discussion, is that it is the Science of Social Anthropology which needs to be used as a resource in investigating what I have attempted to put forward as the deculturalisation of the English People.

The Government of the United Kingdom is without doubt advised by experts in many fields, but I get the strong impression that there is a lack of available expertise in this very vital direction at a time when it is urgently needed as a background to policy-making at the highest level. And I suspect that in part, the reason for this is an academic tendency to subordinate the Science of Social Anthropology to that of Sociology when the very reverse ought to be true.

2. Some main markers of cultural restabilisation

Although I am not myself an academically qualified social anthropologist, much as I should like the chance to engage in formal studies in the discipline, I do understand that one of the results of such studies has been to indicate a series of principal elements which most human societies of most kinds seem to include. This being so, it would seem to be a safer situation were all these principal characteristics of human society to be well represented in modern English society. I think that I have already urged that they are not.

These principal elements that recur with high constancy can be listed:-

a. The formation on a traditional pattern of family and clan relationship patterns, together with the customs of entering into and maintaining the married state after courtship and betrothal.

   Along with this, and closely connected with it, is the tendency of Man to want to live in stable communities, or in tribal structures in more archaic societies.

b. In each human society, there is a recognised way in which the society as a whole is related to the lands on which they live; in which they are distributed within that territory; and in which individuals and families have assigned to them the right to benefit from the fruits of the land.

c. Human societies generally have a set of tests of recognition of entry into adult status, and these tests have the multiple function of ensuring the transmission of basic skills and knowledge from generation to generation; and also of ensuring recognition of the status of adult both within the age group and within the society as a whole.

d. Each human society, while not necessarily having exclusive claim to a particular language, will develop it so that it becomes a perfect medium for expression of the beliefs and values of that society; for the teaching and learning of the necessary skills within their economy; for the adjustment of human relationships; and as a cultural medium for the arts of verbal form, such as musically-accompanied saga.

e. Every human society will have a set of beliefs; concepts of right and wrong; concepts of the origin of the universe and of the Earth; concepts about the nature of things; beliefs about the relationship between the physical order and the invisible order; ideas about the relative importance of things; and other ways of thinking in common about ultimate and often unanswered questions.

These beliefs act as a framework of thought on the basis of which, and within the bounds of which, the individuals of that society can converse with each other secure in the knowledge that they do have a lot in common as a shared background to each particular discussion. Moreover, since these questions are usually faced in the context of a particular formal religion, the individual can also rest secure in the knowledge that when things go disastrously wrong he will have a refuge at least in spirit, till the storm be overpast, or perhaps a death with a meaning that he can face calmly and nobly.

Typically, however, it was not just individuals who were sustained and guided by the religion of the people in question, but the people as a whole, corporately, who sometimes had to face disaster together and – as a people – to maintain the cult and observances of the religion in public fora.

It is not comfortable to live in a society which has no shared beliefs, values, or fundamental concepts. It is not a normal human situation.

f. Normally, a human society has a cultural stock deriving from a classical period, an early time when the culture of the people was taking shape with a certain vigour and unity of spirit which fostered a spontaneous outpouring of creativity.

There will also, typically, be an appeal to an even earlier 'heroic' phase, when with great urgency the people in question had to establish themselves against powerful opposition under the leadership of warrior chieftains whose deeds would then be recounted by saga through the generations long before the people learnt to read and write.

g. Deriving largely from those early times, a particular people will have a range of survival skills and modes of athletic prowess which in part will have been suggested by the terrain in which they lived in the early days. Such skills would normally make it extremely difficult for an enemy to invade their territory, and it is this sort of territorial tenacity which is the primary meaning of the word 'defence'.

Most peoples, too, have their own form of martial arts skills, and skill in the handling of low-technology weaponry of an easily-fabricated sort. It would seem, for example, that the Anglo-Saxons knew of something like the Australian Aboriginal spear-thrower.

h. Marriage has already been mentioned, but a viable human civilisation has, too, a set of shared customs concerned with birth and death: with entry into the world and with the end of this earthly, physical life. The beliefs, of course, will be bound up with the prevailing religion, but there are cultural expressions of these events within the family and the community which are independent of the credal assumptions, and complement the latter.

i. Clearly, whatever a civilisation or a people may have received from the past, they will certainly, unless something is terribly wrong, have a current expression of their collective creativity in a number of directions. The Arts must be alive. It is not enough for a people to become a living folk museum, or to be mere critics of the work of their ancestors.

j. The pattern of subsistence of a people in traditional times and in most human cultures is typically wholly integral to the way of life of the people concerned. Until modern times it was unheard of for there to be a clear-cut division between the economy which supported a people and the way of life which they led. The Modern Economy has taken that schism to extremes.

k. Lastly, in human societies generally there is a stability which obviates the need for a generation gap and renders the concept of 'progress' meaningless. Change there may be, according to the cycles of change of climate, but usually it would be almost imperceptibly slow. Moreover, even where change was perceived, there would be no reason to think that it was irreversible, and where change occurred of a catastrophic nature, those involved would reasonably expect that the phase of rapid change would soon cease and settle down to a new normality. Thus, where a river changed course, where a volcano exploded, where a new and fearsome tribe arrived, a new pattern of things would result which would have its own stability, not necessarily more 'advanced' than the previous one. Such, I think was the case with the Norman Conquest. At least, in its immediate aftermath.

Having thus listed what I believe to be salient markers within cultures and civilisations in general, it would be tempting to suggest ways in which the cultural reconstruction of the English People could begin to proceed. This, however, would be to pre-empt a process in which, as I have said, qualified and experienced social anthropologists are needed to act as a resource to the Government as a background to policy decisions in most major departments. It would also be to repeat much of what I have been attempting to present in a book on the subject of the Modern Civilisation.

Instead, I will allow myself at this point to put in a plea that Her Majesty's Government encourage the preparation of teaching material in the classical language of the English People and also the widespread dissemination of the cultural treasures set forth in that tongue.

And along with that, a second plea that, alongside the Scottish Office and the Welsh Office, there should be an English Office to handle certain matters pertaining to the well-being of the English People as such.

Indeed, as I make this second plea, I wonder how much recognition is accorded to the English People in our legal system. The term 'Great Britain', beyond its ancient territorial sense, refers to a Union of specific peoples which took place in its more definitive phase in 1707. The English People, like the other peoples within the Union, are of very much more ancient origin. It would be reassuring to know that there were some legal recognition of our status as a distinct People. The setting in being of a specifically English Office would be a step towards that.

In Conclusion

This paper is an attempt to bring to the fore what I believe to be a major matter of urgent national importance, and one with very many interconnected aspects in just about every department of human affairs.

My reason for thinking that I should write in this vein was certainly not any belief that I am particularly clever – I have had many years to learn otherwise – but rather that I have had a strange sequence of situations in a number of contrasting countries and cultures, causing me to reflect much more upon the deep roots of human existence in society than is usually the case.

And what I observed upon my return to the United Kingdom not long ago disturbed me very much, and continues so to do.

The salient points that I have herewith urged in some detail are these:-

a. In some parts of the world a grave threat to human existence in society and to the health of the individual has come to light, largely as a result of the inherent instability of the Modern Civilisation. This threat is what I have called deculturalisation.

b. This phenomenon, which denotes the fragmentation, dissipation, and ultimate loss of the human patterning which we call a 'civilisation' or a 'culture', is something with which the English People are threatened very gravely at the present time.

c. I strongly suspect that HM Government lack advice from the necessary quarter in order to investigate and to confront the implications of deculturalisation among the English People and other peoples with British Nationality.

d. The necessary human intellectual discipline is that of Social Anthropology, but the present writer suspects that this discipline, in academic circles, may have suffered something of an eclipse, and may have become wrongfully subordinated to Sociology.

e. I have tentatively supplied a list of salient matters which fairly constantly occur in a wide range of human civilisations and cultures, since it is clear that if these matters are resolved in most civilisations in one way or another it is relevant to pay urgent attention to the question as to whether we resolve them ourselves. It is here that the expertise of the Social Anthropologist will begin to prove important.

Since I am an Anglican priest, originally ordained within the Diocese of Newcastle, England in 1962, it is necessary for me to point out that this letter is written purely in my personal capacity. Currently, I am licensed to operate within the Scottish Episcopal Diocese of Moray, Ross and Caithness, but I am not on the payroll of that Diocese, being rather a non-stipendiary priest working as a hospital gardener at the present time. (1988)

I wish also to point out that I belong to no organisation or pressure group, though I am deeply interested in the subject of human civilisations and cultures, with special reference to how the Modern Civilisation should be best understood.

There are those who expect governments and ministers of the Crown to wave magic wands and make everything perfect with a perfection which they have already defined within the nebulous clouds of their own imagination.

I am not one of those. Rather, being aware of many of the terrible problems which confront the Government at the present time, I should like to be reassured (as currently I am not) that the correct conceptual tools are at hand for the Government Departments to use, and that theoretical advice is being sought from the right quarter.

If the theoretical basis is the correct one, then, no matter how intractable may seem the difficulties and malfunctions of our human society, there is very real hope that Government decisions, made against that background, will lead to satisfactory conclusions in the long run. Conversely, a wrong theoretical base will cause a systematic distortion of Government Policy, no matter how wise and able may be the individual personages concerned and responsible.

The English People first had the Christian Gospel preached to them at the end of the fifth century of our era. From our own ranks rose Hilda, Willibrord, Winfrith and Wulfstan. Cedd, Alfric and Etheldreda. Cuthbert was surely the original patron saint of The English.

I think that it will be accepted and understood if I here voice my belief that the One God and Father of all things who brought His Kingdom and Salvation to The English People so many long years ago will even now hear those of that people who now call upon Him in the same way, through the Gospel of Christ.

It is my prayer that the English People may again become a people who will put their trust in God and of Him be aware of His Protection and innumerable Blessings. And in this way become instrumental in bringing God's Blessing upon many others.

An Afterword (July 1999)
Some thoughts after thirteen years have elapsed

The paper on Deculturalisation was written while I was in Scotland, in 1986, and I now append some thoughts some thirteen years later. I will not attempt to give a résumé of events which have occurred in the intervening period, but rather indicate my present perspective about what things are urgent and necessary to say at the present time.

Cultural Collapse

It is more urgent than ever to recognise the many and various manifestations of cultural collapse, and how they interact and reinforce one another. Human beings are not animals, and we cannot rely solely on instinct; we need a particular culture to belong to, inherited and transmitted, so that we may be secure in the knowledge that we share a particular way of life and mode of thinking with others of our own human society, and so that the word 'we', indeed, has meaning.

These days, we tend to put things in mental and administrative compartments, such as mental illness, lack of preventative medicine, high incidence of crime, obesity and bad diet, dependence on the Social Services, linguistic impoverishment and degradation, inner-city and 'estate' sub-cultures, graffiti, etc., etc.; but in reality all these things are interactive aspects of cultural collapse in an anthropological sense, and there are many more components of this phenomenon. The large-scale confusion about and rejection of historically-rooted religion is also a very important factor.

The Political System

The political system in the United Kingdom is not unaffected by cultural confusion, as there are indications in some quarters of a desire to push the constitution in an American direction, while others would press for increasing integration with the continental EU at all levels. Perhaps the mass of the populace vacillates unthinkingly between the two.

There has also been an ongoing tendency for many functions in society to be undertaken by private companies rather than by the State or by Local

71

Authority departments. But private companies have their own cultures, and are often based elsewhere in the world. The global free market has become a sort of 'god' in the minds of many.

But time was when State governments saw their task as governing peoples and nations, whereas now one can be forgiven for thinking that the main task of government is seen to be that of regulating the parameters of operation for the local sector of the global free-market economy. In such a political climate, the need of the English people (or any other ethnic community in the UK) to reconstruct their culture, rediscover their origins and roots, and express their common identity in currently appropriate ways, becomes increasingly marginalised: it does not matter who we are or what we believe or where we come from, it seems, as long as we fit into the economy.

National Identity

There remains a basic confusion about national identity. It would seem that in the public mind, as expressed in the Press and in the Media, there is a failure to recognise these salient points:–

a   There is no British culture or identity. Britain is a state, a complex assemblage of political machinery and constitutional apparatus, and it now comprises a number of particular cultures and ethnic communities, of which the English People – at least, those who continue to remain in Britain – remain the historically indigenous one.

b   The English People need to be recognised, and to recognise themselves, as the historically indigenous ethnic group in what is still called England.

c   The English, insofar as they recognise their origin, identity and cultural roots, are not 'Westerners', but an ancient northern people.

d   English national identity can be exported, and whereas many British citizens retain a national identity from elsewhere in the world, so too may English people live in a country other than Britain, and may not have British or EU citizenship.

Since the confusion about national identity is found at the highest levels in the political system, it is hard to escape the conclusion that such confusion is being deliberately sustained, as pretensions to particular cultures and identities are no longer convenient within the global free-market economy.

The Plurality of Human Culture – A vitally important concept

It may be taken as unquestionable that until very recently, and even now to a very large degree, the inhabitable world was covered by, as it were, a 'patchwork quilt' of contrasting human cultures, all of which addressed the same basic and fundamental human needs but did so in widely different ways.

This fact may seem obvious, but the importance of it may be overlooked. There is a parallel to be drawn here with the continuing necessity of retaining the wild strains, in all ,their natural diversity, of the vegetables, fruits and grains which we have cultivated in highly specialised ways.

Furthermore, the time-scale needs to be kept in mind: it may take hundreds if not thousands of years for a human culture to develop, but it can be destroyed completely within a few years.

The Importation of American Culture

The massive input from American culture continues, and is exacerbated by the recently devised electronic communication systems with computer databases. Moreover, there is a very great pressure on Britain to become an increasingly open market for American products, including those which might be called mind-shaping.

To take an example. When I was a schoolboy, during and just after the Second World War, there were English comics to read. They were compulsively good reading, they were about English culture and way of life, and they were written in excellent English. The better comics were an education in their own right, and even the lighter ones did no harm and were rather fun. One may well ask what sort of comics are being read now, what culture they are promoting, and what might be the effect of them on young English people who pick them up.

Recently I complained that when I visit the High Street I seem to see, no longer young English people (ethnic minorities apart), but young urban Americans. The person to whom I was talking tried to reassure me by saying that beneath the surface they were still English, but that is rather like looking down a smart shopping mall in Perth WA and saying 'yes, but if you look beneath the surface you'll find it is still basically an Aboriginal society'.

A Purple Movement?

At the end of the 'sixties we had the Ecological Movement, which is still developing with increasing urgency on many fronts.

And just as the Ecological, or Green, Movement drew our attention to the fact that the modern techno-commercial civilisation is destroying the Earth, so too we need a parallel Anthropological Movement in order to draw attention to the fact that the same modern techno-commercial civilisation is destroying human societies. Whimsically, but who knows? Perhaps such a movement could be called the Purple Movement. It has yet to come into being, whatever colour scheme we choose.

Should such a movement come into being, the process of recalling the English People to an awareness and love of their own cultural roots will be part of a much wider rediscovery of what it means to be human.

The Spiritual Dimension

The above sub-heading will ring alarm bells with some, but I cannot in all honesty refrain from saying something about the place of the spiritual in human society, and for English ears in particular. I will make the following observations.

a. Those peoples who happen to have a strong shared spiritual base for their culture and national identity are fortunate indeed. I think of the Armenians, and even more obviously, the Greeks. Where would these two nations be now, were it not for the two respective rites of Christianity (in this case) that held their cultures together for centuries in very hostile conditions?

    As I have remarked elsewhere, the English People, both before and after the Conversion, had a common spiritual base which, whatever other merits the two different religions had respectively, served as a foundation for the English culture and way of life.

b. For want of anything better in modern England we must accept that there continues to be a plurality in which English people find themselves divided between various rites of Christianity, agnosticism, and – in some cases – a sincere seeking for a reconstruction of the ancient heathen religion. (I do not regard 'heathen' as in any way pejorative, but rather as denoting the original indigenous religions that were integral to the cultures of the Northern peoples such as the Early English.)

Agnosticism presents a problem because it is rather an 'umbrella' term. There is that agnosticism which represents a sincere puzzlement in the face of the conflicting claims of religions and rites, and a continuing lack of readiness to accept any of them. What I think is less acceptable is a form of agnosticism which refuses to accept that the human quest for the spiritual is in any way important, for this seems to fly in the face of human experience generally, and overlooks the often agonising need for spiritual guidance on the part of countless ordinary people who yearn for spiritual counsel and reassurance. Similarly, I would regard as questionable that dogmatic brand of agnosticism which would seem to be saying that the quest for the spiritual is meaningless. Meaningless to whom?

c. Faced, then, with the plurality of the English situation, I think that there has to be a comity of religions and rites, along with those who hold to non-religious positions, whereby we agree to work together to reconstruct English culture now, with a respect for the religious situation as we know it to have been in Early English times, both before and after the Conversion.

d. English Christianity has had a stormy and tortuous history in the second millennium, and since the Christian Faith takes its origin in the Eastern Mediterranean at the beginning of the first millennium it behoves Christians of all brands to ask themselves whether they are being true to the original. I make this point because there has been a lot of pressure, recently, tending to make churches conform to the latest trends of our modern 'Western' way of life, and a number of blatantly American forms of sectarianism have been operating in England, seeming to peddle the American way of life more than the Christian Gospel.

In short, it is the task of a religion to be true to its origin, so that whatever spiritual insights, truth, revelation and the like that it had in the first instance may be transmitted through the generations so as to be available for use by all. So did the Australian Aborigines refresh their memories by celebrating the 'Dreamtime' in their corroborees, and reconnect themselves with what happened in the beginning.

For these reasons, the predominant and historically-rooted religion, or religions, in a human society are in a position, not only to provide an ever fresh and unsullied source of basic values and springs of creativity, not to mention solace to individuals in times of grief and sorrow, but more publicly also to act as a flywheel, as it were, holding society together in times of stress, change, and hostile pressure from outside.

So must it be for the English People. We urgently need, as a people, to regain contact with the beginnings of our society, and for this purpose, those religions and rites of Christianity which evince a readiness to renew themselves from their original sources, and at the same time to resist accommodation to the ephemeral cultural pressures for change inherent in the modern techno-commercial civilisation, have a vital and central role to play in the rediscovery and reconstruction of English culture at the present time.

I have written here as one who has needed, and continues to need, the sort of help that only a well-grounded religion can provide. Unreservedly, I am willing to live alongside people whose sources of help and inspiration are other than my own, as long as those sources have antecedents and origins that I can recognise and respect. Moreover, I do not think that it is possible, in the long term, to have a viable human society without a spiritual dimension. So what I am saying here, above all, is that this issue, of the spiritual dimension of our culture, is an important one – centrally important – and it must not be shied away from or buried or neglected.

And Finally

I have written so many words. What I need to do now, and I hope that many others feel the same, is to go to some remoter parts of our English countryside and to reflect on what are the needs of the English People at the present time, as well as to be thankful for what we have received from the past. Within my own spiritual tradition I have made up a short prayer for the English People, and others may do the same according to their own beliefs and traditions. Such reflection, perhaps in prolonged solitude, or with companions of like mind, behoves us all, and the times of silence are often the most fruitful times of all in the long run. So may it be for us who rejoice in being English.

Other Titles – Spring 2000

To be or not to be: The Plight of the English-American
Garman Lord

An English Nationalism
Tony Linsell

For details of these and other titles please write to:

Athelney
1 Providence Street
King's Lynn
Norfolk
PE30 5ET

Þa Engliscan Gesiðas
The English Companions

Þa Engliscan Gesiðas aims to promote a wider interest in, knowledge of and affection for all aspects of Early English culture and tradition. It is a fellowship that enables those with an interest in the early period of English history to exchanging ideas and information with other enthusiasts. The Fellowship publishes a quarterly journal, *Wiðowinde*, which covers all aspects of the Old English period, its language, culture and traditions.

By these means, Þa Engliscan Gesiðas is helping to create a common fund of information and enthusiasm and thereby breathe new life into our native language, literature and art.

Þa Engliscan Gesiðas is a non-political cultural organisation. Membership is open anyone who has an interest in first millennium English history, culture and language.

Further information from:

Ða Engliscan Gesiðas, BM Box 4336, London WC1N 3XX

Website www.kami.demon.co.uk/gesithas/index.html

www.tha-english

www.tha-engliscan-gesithas.org.uk/index.html